I HAVE
BECOME ALIVE

Secrets of the Inner Journey

D0958152

SWAMI MUKTANANDA

A SIDDHA YOGA PUBLICATION
PUBLISHED BY THE SYDA FOUNDATION

Published by SYDA Foundation, 371 Brickman Rd.
South Fallsburg, New York 12779, USA

Edited by Swami Durgananda
Cover design by Cheryl Crawford

First published 1985. Second edition 1992
Second printing 1995
Printed in the United States of America

Library of Congress Cataloging-in-Publication Data
Muktananda, Swami, 1908
        I have become alive: secrets of the inner journey / by Swami
Muktananda. — 2nd ed.
        p.   cm.
        Includes bibliographical references and index.
        ISBN 0-911307-26-5
        1. Spiritual life.   2. Gurus.   I. Title.
BL624.M845   1991
294. 5'4—dc20   91-31166
                                                        CIP

CONTENTS

Swami Muktananda

SWAMI MUKTANANDA
and the Lineage of Siddha Yoga Masters

Swami Muktananda was born in 1908 to a prosperous family of landowners near the South Indian city of Mangalore. At around the age of fifteen, he had several encounters with the great saint, Bhagawan Nityananda, whom he would later recognize as his spiritual Master. These encounters were a turning point for the boy. Shortly thereafter, he decided to set out from home in search of direct experience of God, a journey that would ultimately take him three times across the length and breadth of India and last almost a quarter of a century. He met his first teacher, Siddharudha Swami, who was one of the renowned scholars and saints of that time, in an ashram in Hubli, two hundred miles to the north of his parents' home. It was there that he studied Vedanta, took the vows of *sannyasa*, or monkhood, and received the name Swami Muktananda, "the bliss of liberation."

When Siddharudha died, in 1929, Swami Muktananda began to visit one ashram after another, meeting and learning from more than sixty spiritual teachers, always looking for the one who would give him the experience of God. He searched for eighteen years. In that time he mastered the major scriptures of India, received training in an array of disciplines and skills — from hatha yoga to cooking and *ayurvedic* medicine — and still he did not find what he sought.

At last one of the saints he met sent him to Bhagawan Nityananda, the Siddha Master, or perfected spiritual teacher,

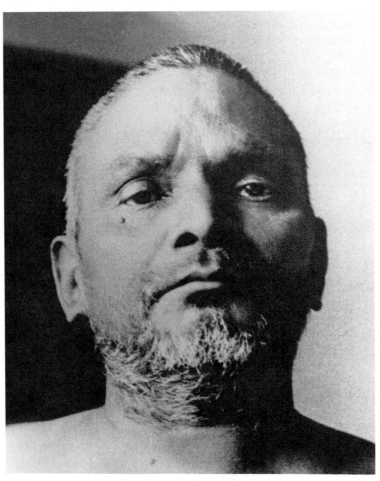

Bhagawan Nityananda

he had encountered so many years before. Bhagawan Nityananda was then living in the tiny village of Ganeshpuri, fifty miles northeast of Bombay. Recognizing Bhagawan Nityananda as the Guru he had been seeking, Swami Muktananda later said that this meeting "ended my wandering forever." From Bhagawan Nityananda he received *shaktipat*, the sacred initiation of the Siddhas by which one's inner spiritual energy is awakened. This energy, known as Kundalini, is a divine potential that exists within each human being; once awakened, it enables a seeker to reach the most subtle levels of inner experience.

With his initiation, Swami Muktananda became a disciple, dedicating himself to the spiritual path set forth by his Guru. This was the beginning of nine years of intense transformation, during which Muktananda underwent total purification, explored the inner realms of consciousness, and finally became steady in his experience of the fullness and ecstasy of his own innermost nature. In 1956 Bhagawan Nityananda declared that his disciple's inner journey was complete: Swami Muktananda had attained Self-realization, the experience of union with God.

Even after he had attained the goal of his discipleship, Swami Muktananda remained a devoted disciple, continuing to live quietly near Ganeshpuri. Bhagawan Nityananda established him in a small ashram near his own, and for five years, Guru and disciple lived less than a mile from each other. Then in 1961, just before his death, Bhagawan Nityananda passed on to Swami Muktananda the grace-bestowing power of the Siddha Masters, investing him with the capacity to give spiritual awakening to others. On that day, Bhagawan Nityananda told him, "The entire world will see you."

In the decades that followed, Baba, as Swami Muktananda came to be known, traveled throughout the world, imparting to others the same *shaktipat* initiation he himself had received and introducing seekers to the spontaneous yoga of the Siddha Masters. He freely bestowed the grace his Guru had given to him, opening to unprecedented numbers of people what he

Swami Chidvilasananda

called "the royal road" of Siddha Yoga — a wide and accessible path to God. People who had never before heard of meditation found that in Baba's presence they were drawn into an inner stillness that gave their lives new focus and meaning. He introduced programs to give *shaktipat* initiation to vast groups and tirelessly explained to people the ongoing process of transformation that was unfolding within them. As Baba became world renowned, his ashram (now known as Gurudev Siddha Peeth) expanded to accommodate the visiting seekers, and in time other ashrams and hundreds of Siddha Yoga Meditation centers were established throughout the world.

In 1982, shortly before his death, Swami Muktananda designated Swami Chidvilasananda his successor. She had been his disciple since early childhood and had traveled with him since 1973, translating into English his writings, his lectures, and the many informal exchanges he had with his devotees. An advanced spiritual seeker from an early age, with a great longing for God, she became an exemplary disciple. She was guided meticulously in her *sadhana* by her Guru, who carefully prepared her to succeed him as Guru. In early May of 1982, Swami Chidvilasananda took formal vows of monkhood, and later that month Swami Muktananda bequeathed to her the power and authority of the Siddha lineage, the same spiritual legacy that his Guru had passed on to him. Since that time, Gurumayi, as she is widely known, has given *shaktipat* and taught the practices of Siddha Yoga to ever-increasing numbers of seekers, introducing them to Swami Muktananda's message:

> *Meditate on your Self.*
> *Honor your Self.*
> *Worship your Self.*
> *Understand your own Self.*
> *God dwells within you as you.*

INTRODUCTION

To live in freedom: this is the exalted goal. Yet spiritual freedom is hard won. We struggle and eventually realize that we must connect with something beyond our small selves in order to achieve it.

The ancient wisdoms of India describe the enlightened one, the Siddha, the *jivanmukta*, who achieves a state of permanent spiritual realization while continuing to live in the world of ordinary mortals. By comparison with the power, vibrancy, and bliss of the liberation that he savors at every moment, the perfected being evaluates ordinary human existence as a state akin to death.

Such a one is the Guru, who comes to temper us, to purify us, and finally to destroy irrevocably our limitations so that we too may become free. Out of compassion and love, the Guru refuses to conspire with us in the cult of our own smallness. By connecting with the true Guru, we become capable of yielding to that which is glorious and real, the true immensity that we are, the astonishing reality.

In India, the god Shiva is traditionally seen as the destroyer who comes with fire at the end of time to destroy the universe of form and the realms of transmigration. On the inner journey, Shiva is the graceful yet relentless destroyer of bondage and of limitation. There are human beings who become so fully free that they may be said to embody the liberating power of Shiva. Such a rare being was Swami Muktananda.

I recall the first time, many years ago, that I saw a photograph of Swami Muktananda. In a university library, on the cover of a

book entitled simply GURU, an amazing face caught my attention
— dignified, intensely alive, brimming with energy and vigor,
yet appealingly gentle. The lips hinted at a contained playfulness.
The eyes, however, were molten furnaces, burning with a sharply
piercing, fierce, and fearless look. It was an entrancing visage,
which, even as I looked at it, seemed to change with quicksilver
fluidity.

Who was it that looked out at me from those eyes? *I Have
Become Alive*, the title of this book, gives us a clue. The divine
"I," the *purnahanta*, the perfectly full and complete Consciousness,
lies concealed within and behind the masks of our ordinary
personality. It is this great "I" who becomes alive for us. This is
the great Self of all beings, the huge and unconstrained light of
universal Consciousness. When it awakens within a human being,
the *jivanmukta* becomes alive. The divine Consciousness of the
universe then gazes out through human eyes into the world of
mortal beings.

In this, his last book, Swami Muktananda's predominant
concern was to express the absolute necessity of spiritual
experience for the living of an authentic life. Using stories, tales,
and traditional examples to illustrate his points, Swami
Muktananda spoke with the unhesitating, authentic voice of
India. Yet he gave expression to the universal truths of life. In his
genial yet uncompromising way he emphasizes again and again:
It is the role of the Guru to bestow freedom by bringing death to
the limited and limiting ego. The Guru's highest task is to
precipitate the death of our constraining ordinariness. He releases
us from suffering and delivers us from the deadly suffocation of a
false existence.

Last year, I spent four months at Gurudev Siddha Peeth, the
ashram that Swami Muktananda built in Ganeshpuri, India. I had
come to study under the direction of Gurumayi Chidvilasananda,
Swami Muktananda's successor as head of the Siddha lineage. As
I went about my tasks in the ashram, I made it a point to pay a
daily visit to Swami Muktananda's Samadhi Shrine, to the place
where he is buried. As I sat in its cool, marbled precincts, I would
be overcome with a powerful surge of inner joy, and invariably, as
I closed my eyes, I would be drawn into a very deep meditation.
Outwardly, I would feel tears of apparently unmotivated happiness
brimming from my eyes. Inwardly, I felt myself touching an
incomparable place of power and wisdom.

Though he no longer inhabits a physical body, Swami Muktananda's beneficent wisdom and initiatory power continue to expand. What I once saw emerging from his eyes, I have now experienced as the liberating gaze of Gurumayi Chidvilasananda. I consider myself exceedingly fortunate to have met her. Like Swami Muktananda before her, she teaches through the contagion of love. To come into the presence of such a being is to fall irrevocably in love. I can say from my own experience that amazing transformation and long-hoped-for inner journeys began when I entered her presence.

When one listens to the Guru speak, it is as if one's own innermost heart is gently and softly whispering life's deepest truths from within. The words of the Guru trigger an extraordinary response. As one recognizes their fundamental and undeniable truth, the speech of the Siddha Guru opens up a dimension of embodied divinity in which all things shine in the unhindered light of the Self.

I Have Become Alive introduces one to these exquisite vistas of experiential wisdom. Its teachings have the capacity to change lives. As you read it, you will catch a glimpse of an extraordinary power. Taste this power of grace, of *shaktipat*, the inner awakening that so richly flows from these pages. Taste the real energy of life that will begin to surge within you. And then allow it to make you free, to make you come alive!

PAUL E. MULLER-ORTEGA
DEPARTMENT OF RELIGIOUS STUDIES
MICHIGAN STATE UNIVERSITY
JANUARY 28, 1991

The Ego and The Self

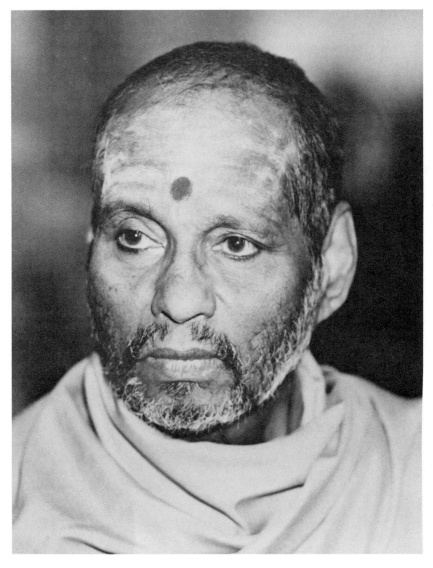

Swami Muktananda

I Have Become Alive

Human life is sublime. It is mysterious and worth knowing. It is the blossoming flower of happiness, the flame of God. But only to a person who really lives does life reveal its mystery. Life is great only for a person who is truly alive. What does it mean to be truly alive? To be truly alive means to know your own Self, to know the Consciousness that pervades everywhere in the universe and lives within the human heart. A person who does not recognize his own Self, a person who identifies with his body, a person who thinks that only worldly life is real and that God does not exist—such a person is not really living.

Once I read the story of a princess. One day, when she was eighteen or nineteen years old, she took off her clothes and began to go naked around the palace. Many methods were tried to cure her, but no matter what anyone did or said, she would not put on any clothes. Her parents consulted physicians. They worshipped all the deities. They sent for holy men to practice different mantras and tantras. But nothing that anyone did could change the condition of the princess.

Then one morning a great yogi happened to pass by the palace. He stood outside the gate to ask for alms, repeating the mantra *Alak Niranjina. Alak Niranjina* means "I am that supreme Principle which is totally pure and cannot be perceived by the senses." The moment the princess heard those words, she called to her friends, "Hurry and bring me my clothes!" She put on a saree and ornaments. Then she went to the kitchen and got some food, gave it to the yogi, and returned to her room.

The king was bewildered by his daughter's actions. He asked her "O my daughter, for so many days you have stayed naked. No matter how much money we spent, no matter how much worship we did, no matter how many mantras we repeated, you would not put on clothes. What happened today?"

"O father," said the princess. "Should I tell you the truth? Some time ago I realized that I was without knowledge of the Self and that, without that knowledge, I was as good as dead. That is why I gave up my clothes. Since I was a dead person surrounded by other dead people, why did I need clothes? When a person is dead, what shame does he have? But when I saw that yogi, I realized that he knew the Truth, and that he was fully alive. Therefore, I felt ashamed to be naked in his presence, and so I put on my clothes."

There is great meaning in the words of the princess. The great being Rama Tirth said, "O God, unless I know You, I am not truly living." St. John of the Cross said, "I live without inhabiting myself, in such a wise that I am dying that I do not die." When a person is far away from the Self, how can he be said to be alive? A person who does not have the inspiration of the Self, a person who considers himself different from the Self, is not a living being at all. He is dead, buried under a thick blanket of ignorance.

The sages, the philosophers, the scriptural authors, and all the saints have told us this again and again. With great love, they have tried to awaken us, to shake us out of our ignorance. But even when they shake us, even when they try to pull the blanket away from our bodies, we keep hugging the blanket. We put one blanket over another on top of ourselves, and we never want to let our blankets go. Still, the great beings keep telling us, "O Self-forgetful one, wake up, wake up. At least now, listen to me. The state of the Self, the knowledge of the Self, the wisdom of the Self is very easy to attain. Turn inward and perceive That. This world which you think is real is fleeting, temporary. Soon all the things which seem so real to you will perish."

When the saints say these things to us, we wonder what they mean. After all are we not awake now? It is true that the world seems very real to us, but when we are asleep and dreaming, the world of our dreams also seems very real. When a snake bites us in our dream, we weep and wail and feel that we are dying. Yet when we wake up from that dream, the snake no longer exists. In the same way, when we wake up from the long dream that is our life, we will realize that what we think is a world is not a world at all, but an appearance of Consciousness, an emanation of God. As soon as we know the truth about ourselves, we will understand that we are not this body made of flesh and blood. We will realize that we are not limited individual souls, but something else. We will know that we are nothing but God.

In the *Chandogya Upanishad*, the sage Uddalaka told Svetaketu, "In that subtle essence, all things have their existence. That is the Self. You are That." No matter who we may think we are, no matter what country we may come from, no matter which language we may speak, we all have within us the same "I"-consciousness. When you are born, you are only that "I," that pure being. But immediately, people begin to superimpose different kinds of understanding on that original "I." In the beginning, your "I" was perfectly clean and clear, but just as you would add colors to water, you add different things to that "I." And as soon as you add these colors to the "I," you make it impure. Then, instead of identifying yourself as that Consciousness, you consider yourself to be man or woman. You consider yourself to belong to a particular family or caste. You consider yourself to be intelligent or stupid, superior or inferior, a great person or a small one, a virtuous person or a sinful one. If you study a little, you consider yourself learned, and if you do not study anything, you consider yourself illiterate. Likewise, when anger, greed, attachment, and desires arise inside of you, you identify yourself with them and feel that you are one with those emotions. You identify yourself with the body and the experiences of the mind and senses. Then, caught in the net of these different identifications you flounder in the current of worldly life, sometimes experiencing pleasure and sometimes experiencing pain, sometimes happiness and sometimes sorrow. In this way, you go through life becoming one thing or another but never becoming what you are.

There is a story in the Puranas, the mythological books of India, which illustrates how powerful that net of false identification can be. Once there were two demons, Shumba and Nishumba. They had been given the boon that they could not be killed by anybody in the world, except each other. Since they were brothers and loved each other, the question of their killing each other could never arise. So they thought that they were above death, and as a result they had become completely drunk with pride. A person who is mad with pride does not realize what the consequences of his pride might be. In the fit of pride he may say, "I'll do this, and I'll do that." He might say, "No one can do anything to me," but he does not know what the consequences of his situation might be. There was a saint who was asked what death is, and he said, "The only death I know is the death of one's own ego, one's own conceit, one's own arrogance. There is no other death." This was exactly the state of Shumba and Nishumba; they were inviting their own death by their own conceit. They began to persecute people. They had no pity or compassion, and they would torment people in whatever way they wanted. When people could not take it any longer, they went to Lord Vishnu and prayed to him to save them. Vishnu heard their prayers and agreed to help them, but he realized that nobody else could kill Shumba and Nishumba, that they could only kill each other. As he was wondering what to do, he had a brainstorm. He took the form of a beautiful woman. In that form he was so fascinating and entrancing that everyone who saw him became bewitched by him. Even his name, Mohini, meant "the one who infatuates." In the form of Mohini, Vishnu descended into the forest where the two demons lived. Mohini began to walk toward their house, and as she walked, even the rocks and trees began to sway with love for her. At last, Mohini arrived at the demons' house. She sat down between them. First she looked at Shumba. Then she looked at Nishumba. Immediately, both demons fell in love with her. They forgot all about beating and robbing people. All they could think about was Mohini. "Mohini, marry me," said Shumbha. "No, marry me," said Nishumbha.

Mohini laughed. "I can't marry both of you," she said. "I can marry only one."

"Which one will you marry?" the demons asked.

"I will marry the one who is stronger," she replied.

Without another word, the demons began to fight. They were so fierce and powerful that the whole forest shook with the force of their battle. They fought and fought, but neither of them could defeat the other. Finally, both of them died.

When Mohini looked at the two dead demons lying on the ground, she thought to herself, "Those two demons died for love of me! How beautiful I must be!" She ran to a nearby stream and looked at her reflection in the water. As soon as she saw herself, she became just as bewitched by her beauty as the demons had been. "Wow, wow, I am so gorgeous," she said. "No one can compare with me!" There is an aphorism in the *Pratyabhijnahridayam*, the great text of Kashmir Shaivism, which explains that when Consciousness becomes deluded by its own powers and forgets its true nature, the supreme Lord becomes an individual soul. This is what had happened to Mohini. She was so fascinated by herself that she forgot that she was really Vishnu, the supreme Lord. "What a shame that such a beautiful girl should be all alone!" she thought. "I need a husband!" So Mohini set off through the forest, looking for the right man to marry. She wandered from place to place, until finally she grabbed hold of somebody who agreed to marry her. While preparations for the wedding were being made, the great sage Narada arrived. When he saw Vishnu in the guise of Mohini, he realized what had happened. "Look, if you were really a girl it would be all right for you to marry this boy," he said, "but how can a boy marry another boy? Don't you remember who you are?"

We are in exactly the same predicament as Lord Vishnu. We are the Lord, yet we have forgotten our true nature and have become Mohinis. We are the great Self, but we have been trapped by the delusion of ego, and as a result we have become limited individual souls. This is the state which the great beings have called ignorance. This is the state of bondage.

We do not realize how the ego deludes us. It is that limited "I"-sense, the false individual ego, which gives rise to the notion within us that the Self, which is in reality deathless, immutable, and eternal, was born at a certain time and will die at a certain time. It is that ego which has made us small and which jealously guards our smallness, because it knows that if our smallness were to go, it too would have to go. The ego lives within us masquerading as our best friend, but actually it is our worst enemy. The ego shows us to ourselves in the wrong light. It serves as a screen between our real Self and our understanding. It is due to the ego that we remain far away from the Truth, that we remain separate and alienated from our own Self. It is the ego that has caused our births and deaths of innumerable lifetimes. There is only one bondage, and that is the bondage of ego.

A great being of Maharashtra said, "Man is in such a plight. Because of the ego, he is born in different species and dies, he is born and he dies, yet he neither opens his eyes nor repents." Swami Rama Tirth said, "Because of the ego, a person fails to understand the Truth. He develops so much hatred and hostility, and he makes God's creation hell." In this way, the company of ego is the company of death. It is only when we discard the ego, this false "I"-sense which identifies with this perishable body and thinks that our identity as a man or a woman is who we really are, that we become alive. It is only then that we become free of bondage.

Just as when we get rid of anger, we discover love, when we get rid of the ego, we discover that place within us which is pure Consciousness, which is God.

To give up the ego means to merge it in the bliss of the Self, to dissolve our smallness into the vastness of Consciousness. When bubbles arise on the surface of the ocean, they seem to be different from the ocean, but after a while, the bubbles burst and merge back into the ocean. In the same way, when our bubble of ego bursts, when our sense of limitation leaves us, we will realize that we are nothing but that Consciousness.

Augustine was a great saint of Christianity, who spent his entire life searching for inner peace. He looked for satisfaction in outer sense pleasures. He ate a lot and drank a lot, and tried many other things in life. He also pursued many different spiritual practices, but he always remained dissatisfied. In his search, he passed from one city to another, from one forest to another. He studied every available book on religion and science, until finally his burden of acquired knowledge became intolerably heavy. Yet still he was without peace.

One day as Augustine was walking by the ocean, he saw a boy standing by the shore, holding a cup in his hand. The boy looked very worried and anxious, and Augustine wondered why such a young boy had so much on his mind. So he approached him and asked, "What's the matter with you? Why are you so depressed?"

The boy said, "I am trying to figure out how I can make the ocean come into my cup. But no matter what I do there is no way I can contain the ocean in this cup. The ocean is so big, and my cup is so small."

"Then why don't you just throw your cup into the ocean?" Augustine said. As he said those words, Augustine had a flash of insight. He realized that he was doing exactly the same thing as that boy. He was trying to hold the infinite bliss of God in the tiny cup of his individual "I"-sense. And the moment he realized that, he threw away the cup of his ego. Immediately, he discovered that he could hold the ocean. He realized his oneness with God.

The truth is that we are all like that boy. There are millions and millions of us standing on the shore of the ocean of Consciousness, trying to hold it in our cups. We keep looking at each others' cups and comparing our cups and having arguments about our cups. Some of us feel proud because our cup is bigger than someone else's, and some of us feel jealous because we think someone else's cup is bigger than ours. What we do not realize is that none of our cups can contain the vast ocean of God. If we were to throw our cups into the ocean, if we were to merge our egos into the bliss of God, then we would no longer be crying and wailing in our separate ego-sense. We would be one with that ocean.

The great saint Eknath Maharaj had studied all the scriptures and had also composed great philosophical works. At the end he said, "Now I will show you the master key by which you can see God immediately. When you give up the ego, all that is left is God."

It is only because of the ego that we have to do *sadhana*, or spiritual practice. It is to destroy the ego, the sense of separation and individuality, that we meditate. It is to destroy the ego that we practice yoga. It is to destroy the ego that we go to the Guru. Otherwise, there would be no need for us to do any of these things. We do not have to attain God, because we are already God. God pervades every pore of our bodies, every cell of our blood, and every particle of the dust of this earth. Yet we cannot know that all-pervasive great Being unless we destroy our sense of separateness, our individuality. An ecstatic being wrote, "When a seed is sown in the earth, it loses its individuality inside the earth. Yet after a while, it sprouts and becomes a beautiful plant." Only by losing its individuality can the seed grow into a plant. In the same way, only by merging our limiting ego into the Self can we grow into the Self.

As long as the ego is alive, we are limited mortal creatures. We go from death to death, being born only to die and dying in order to be reborn. But when the ego dies, when our sense of limitation is no more, our death also dies, and we become immortal. In meditation, through the grace of the Guru, there comes a moment when we come face to face with our own death. That moment, when the ego dies in meditation, is also the death of our death. Once we have seen our own death with our own eyes, once we have died in the Self, we will never die again. Jesus said, "By losing yourself you shall find yourself; by dying you shall live." Another great being described it very well in one of his poems. He said, "When I met the pure One, I became pure. My ego was erased, and I became God."

Don't Become Anything

Once a Guru and his disciple were traveling together. As they traveled on their journey, the Guru would tell the disciple, "Never become anything. If you don't become anything, you will never experience any trouble."

They kept walking through the forest until one day they came to the guest house in which the king of that place used to stay while on long hunting trips. They went inside and were very happy to find a beautiful room with two comfortable beds. "Guruji, is it all right if we sleep here?" the disciple asked. "It's fine," said the Guru, "but make sure that while you are sleeping you don't become anything." "Why should I become anything while I'm asleep?" the disciple wondered. He lay down on one bed, and the Guru lay down on the other. Soon they were sleeping with great joy.

Now it happened that the king was on a hunting trip that day and was using the guest house. When he returned from his hunting trip with his guards, he was amazed to see two ragged travelers snoring away on the magnificent royal beds. The king walked over to the Guru and shook him. The old man opened his eyes and looked at him, then closed them and pretended to fall back to sleep. The king shook him a second time and asked, "Who are you? Where did you come from? What do you want?" The old man said nothing. The king thought that he must be a half-wit. "Take him out of here and put him under a tree," he told the guards.

Then the king went to the other bed and shook the disciple. Once again he asked, "Who are you? What are you doing here?" The disciple was startled and forgot what his Guru had told him. He replied, "You should know better than to talk to me so rudely. I am a swami of the Saraswati order and the disciple of a great Guru."

The king was very offended. He said, "You are a rascal and your Guru must also be a rascal." He ordered the guards to whip the disciple twenty-one times and to throw him out the front door. Tears began to flow out of the eyes of the young *yogiraj*, but they were not tears of devotion; they were tears of pain.

As he lay moaning in the street in front of the guest house, the disciple saw the Guru lying peacefully under a tree. He dragged himself over to the Guru and woke him up. Then he began to complain, "O Guruji, they whipped me so savagely. They even kicked me with their boots. I am totally covered with sores. Why didn't your grace protect me?"

The Guru replied, "Why did they beat you? They didn't beat me. They gently lifted me up and laid me here on the ground. If you had followed my instructions, then my grace would certainly have protected you. You must have become something. What did you say to them?"

The disciple said, "I told them that I was the disciple of a great Guru."

The Guru replied, "It is just as I thought. I warned you that if you became anything you would get into trouble. Because I did not claim to be anything, nobody did anything to me."

It is the ego which makes life whip you remorselessly. If you are like the disciple and add something to the pure "I," you receive blows. If you are like the Guru and remain just that pure Self, then nothing in the world can harm you.

What Is the Ego?

Q: How can I use my ego creatively?

SM: Let us forget about using it creatively. Instead, let us examine the ego from an analytical point of view and try to see what there really is in it. Once a seeker put a similar question to a seer, and the seer replied, "You are attaching your ego to this body, which is perishing every moment, which is full of all kinds of fluids, and from which waste matter is constantly coming out. What is there in the body which could serve as a basis for your ego? This body is made from the sexual fluid of your father and mother. When your body comes from your parents, you surely cannot take pride in owning it. Even after you are born, your body is sustained by the food which grows from the earth. There is no basis for pride in that either. You see through the eyes which have been given by God, you hear through the ears which have been given by God, you speak with the tongue which is a gift of God, so why should you take pride in your senses? How can you keep saying 'I, I, I' when this is so? When the consciousness dwelling inside this body leaves it, then the body is taken to a cemetery and buried. It is completely worthless. So is there any basis in the body for one's ego?"

My Guru used to speak in a strange way. He would say few words, but those words were very mysterious. Because he lived close to Bombay, thousands of people would come to see him. When a person goes somewhere, what does he take with him? He takes his own worthiness, his own wealth. When a singer goes somewhere, he always sings. Singing is his wealth. No matter where a writer goes, he always wants to find something to write about. Writing is his wealth. No matter where an actor goes, he always emotes, because acting is his wealth. When a poet goes somewhere, even if he's driving a car, he composes, because poetry is his wealth. Every person carries his own goal, his own purpose.

When people came to see my Baba, they always carried their own wealth, their own bundle. The saints always say, "If you ever go to meet a *sadhu*, a holy being, leave your ego outside, just as you would your shoes. Don't you ever take your ego inside." But when people from Bombay came to see my Baba, they would bring their egos with them, and their egos would never allow them to understand what my Baba really was.

Usually my Baba would lie on his cot, and if he turned his face to one side, it would take him three or four hours to turn to the other side. It is said, "A person who has become lazy about opening and closing his eyes is the true king of enlightened beings." But the people who went to see my Baba did not understand his state. When he would turn away like that, their egos would start growling and they would begin to burn inside. They would mutter, "What kind of swami is he? Why doesn't he speak to us?" After some time had passed, my Baba would suddenly speak up, and his words were very strong. I sometimes hesitated to use his words in the West, because they were so strong. He would say, "Hey, you pot of shit, why do you have so much pride? Why are you so egotistical about this body?" This is how my Baba used to speak. Of course, I use a more polite term. I call this body a factory of shit. Just as a nylon factory produces nylon, this body produces shit. No matter what you eat, it leaves the body in the form of shit. The scriptural authors say, "This body has nine gates, and filth always comes out of them. If you put your fingers in your nose, dirt comes out. If you put your hand in your ear, dirt comes out." And so the scriptural authors ask, "Why are you so proud of this body? What is so great about this mind? What do you have to be so egotistical about?"

If you have to be ruled by ego, at least let that ego be the proper, the pure ego. When you have a stirring of ego inside, do not condition it with anything else. For instance, when you have the sense of "I" arising within, do not identify it with your name, your body, your clothes. Just stay on the level of the pure "I"-awareness, the "I"-consciousness which has not become identified with other things. That is quite valid. You should identify the ego as *So'ham. Ham* means "I," and *So* means "That," so *So'ham* is the awareness "I am that Consciousness which is the supreme Truth." There is an eternal Principle behind the mind, from which ego arises and which observes ego all the time. Identify yourself with that. That pure "I"-awareness has no appendages. That is the supreme Truth, and that is the right kind of "I"-awareness. The Vedas point to the pure "I"-awareness, the "I"-awareness which is free of all identifications, and they have sanctioned it. The sanction is in the Vedic dictum *Aham brahmasmi*, "I am the highest Being." So change the direction of your ego. Have the ego of "I am Consciousness, I am God, I am pure, I am all-pervasive, I am perfect." That kind of ego is perfectly valid.

Letting Go

Q: How long will it take me to get rid of my ego? It is very stubborn.

SM: As much time as it takes you to snap your fingers. As much time as it takes you to spit. Your ego is not holding you. You are holding it. Once a man went to see King Janaka. He found Janaka standing under a tree. He had put his elbow on a branch, and he was resting his head on his hand, thinking about something. The man asked, "You are Janaka, you are a great king. Not only that, you have risen above body-consciousness. I want your help to discard my ego." Janaka stood there with his arm around the branch and said, "Brother, just wait. I will answer your question when this branch lets me go."

"But the branch is not holding you," the man said. "You are holding that branch."

"You are in the same situation," said Janaka. "It is you who are holding onto your ego. You have made your ego your friend and you don't want to let go of it. Now, all you have to do is let go of it, and you will be free."

The Personality Remaining

Q: How is the personality remaining after the ego is obliterated different from the ego? What is its relation to the inner Self? How are emotions expressed through it different from those expressed through the ego?

SM: When the ego is obliterated, your personality is not obliterated. For instance, if there is a person who gets angry, but his anger leaves him, what makes you think that his personality also leaves him? In the same way, if a person's ego leaves him, what makes you think that his personality also leaves him? His personality will remain. Once the ego leaves, then what is left is the inner Self.

To Become Aware of the Witness

Q: What is the most direct way to be rid of the idea "I am the body"?

SM: Only through the knowledge of the Self can you get rid of the idea "I am the body." After receiving Shakti, as one meditates continually and becomes aware of the inner Truth, this idea begins to fade away. In fact, sometimes one becomes aware that one is not only this body, but everything else, too. Shaivism says that when a man gains full realization of the Truth, he begins to understand that everything in the universe is the glory of his own manifestation.

If you contemplate the constantly changing experiences in your life, or even the states that you pass through every day, the waking state, the dream state, and the deep sleep state, you will come to know that you are completely different from your body. A person who lives in a house is different from the house. He may build this house, he may furnish it, he may live in it, but he always understands that he is different from it. A person who knows an object is different from that object. What illumines something is completely different from the object it illumines. Vedanta says, "The perceiver is completely different from the object of perception." A person says, "This is my body" in the same way that he says, "This is my house." The fact that he uses the possessive indicates that he knows that the body is an object to him. It belongs to him, but it is not him.

Within you there is a being who knows both the waking and dream states, yet remains different from them. He witnesses all the actions that take place in the waking state. Even when you are asleep and dreaming, there is a being who remains different from your dream state, a witness who remains awake and reports your dream to you when you wake up. Have you ever wondered who remembers your dream state? While you are sleeping, who is awake? If that witness were also sleeping when you are sleeping, then who would know what is happening in your dreams? If that being is not sleeping when you are sleeping, then who is he? That being is called Consciousness. That is God. That is the knower who is always fully conscious. That is the inner Self. The Upanishads say that the one who knows the waking state, the dream state, and the deep sleep state, not only that, the one who knows the meshes of the world, is the eternal Principle. To become aware of that witness and to identify yourself with that is the surest way to rid yourself of the idea that you are the body.

When the Ego Goes. . .

There are many techniques for attaining God-realization. Some people conclude that since everyone is involved in one such technique or another, God must be quite far from us and that it will take us a long time to find Him. But all these notions about the difficulty of finding God, about the need to work very hard and to undergo backbreaking tests in order to experience Him, arise from our ego. In one of his poems, the poet-saint Brahmananda said that there was never a time when God was unmanifest. God is manifest everywhere. He is born to everyone. If he seems unmanifest to us, it is because of our ego. Tukaram Maharaj also said that although God is quite apparent, people are blind, and because of their blindness they keep wandering here and there. According to the sage Vasishtha there are only two states: the state of bondage and the state of liberation. The state of bondage is the state in which we are trapped by our ego. The state of liberation is simply the state in which we are without ego.

Not only ordinary people are afflicted by ego. Great people also have egos. Being a small person has one redeeming feature: since the ego of a small person is small, his suffering is also small. But the ego of a great person is enormous, and so his suffering is also great. If a person's ego is small it can be tackled with a little piece of rock, but if it is big you have to use very powerful cannons to destroy it.

In ancient India there was a great seer named Vyasa. His son Shuka was an accomplished yogi who had marvelous powers and great knowledge. He had become *urdhvareta*—his sexual fluid moved only upward. Though he had acquired such vast learning, Shuka was without peace. Vyasa knew about his son's problems, but even though he was such a great Guru, he was helpless to do anything.

One day the father said, "King Janaka, the sovereign of this land, is an extraordinary enlightened being. Though he lives in the body, he is in the state beyond the body. Go and study with him, and he will enable you to become centered in the inner Self." But when Shuka went to King Janaka, he discovered to his horror that the man he was supposed to study with was sitting on a golden throne and wearing a golden crown. Maids and servants were fanning him and seven hundred queens were seated near him. Shuka was a great *avadhut*, a great ascetic. He had achieved the heights of renunciation and wore only a small loincloth. When he saw Janaka he thought, "This king is nothing but a sensualist. What can he teach me?" And he returned to his father. Vyasa asked him, "Did you see King Janaka?"

"Yes," Shuka replied, "but I don't think he can help me. A Guru should be as luminous as the sun, but without its heat. A Guru should be as cool as the moon, but without its stains."

"You saw him with prejudiced eyes," Vyasa said. "Janaka is the greatest sage alive today. There is no one greater. And he is exactly the Guru you have described. Try again, and be a little more sensible this time."

Shuka went back to Janaka's court. Again he was shocked by the royal splendor surrounding the king. For the second time he left and returned to his father. "Did you receive anything?" Vyasa asked.

Shuka replied, "What on earth could I receive there?"

"You must go back and give it another try," said Vyasa.

Again Shuka went to Janaka's court, and again he returned. Each time Shuka returned his father would send him back to the king, saying, "You can get peace only from him." Finally, as Shuka was returning for the ninth time, he encountered an old ascetic, who asked him, "How many visits have you made to the king?"

"Nine," said Shuka.

"Did you see the king as he was, or did you see him according to your own projection?" asked the ascetic. "Shukamuni, know that the Truth is beyond both enjoyment and renunciation. Only a few people know that Truth. One who doubts or criticizes such an enlightened being loses all the merit he might have earned as a result of his past good deeds. Since you have already found fault with Janaka nine times, you have lost most of your merit. Don't be stupid any longer. You can receive knowledge of the Truth only from him." With that, the old ascetic disappeared. The moment Shuka heard these words, he became aware of his stupidity. He realized, "Janaka is a pure being, and because of my ignorance I have projected my own stupidity onto him." He was so shocked that he collapsed. After he had regained consciousness, he went back to the king.

Janaka knew that Shuka was coming and instructed his guard not to let him into the palace. "Let him stand outside for three days," he said. Shuka stood like a log outside the palace for three days. Then Janaka said, "Now, for three days, keep him in the inner palace where all my queens live." He instructed all the queens to take good care of him. Shuka's name had become proverbial for celibacy. During these three days all the queens tried to initiate him in their own way. Some queens bathed him. Others rubbed sandalwood paste on his body. Some kissed him and others hugged him. But he was not at all affected.

Finally, the king sent for him. When Shuka walked into the

court, he was amazed by what he saw. The king was seated on the throne, and his beautiful maidservants were applying sandalwood paste and perfumes to one of his legs and massaging it, while his other leg was lying in the midst of a blazing fire. Since Shuka's ego had progressively diminished and he had become purer, he had become more aware of who King Janaka really was, and he felt more reverence for him. Now he realized that the king was not caught in either renunciation or sensuality. Shuka had thought that the king was a sensualist, but now he realized that he was beyond both. Shuka prostrated before Janaka and said, "Please show me the way to peace."

"Sit down," said Janaka. It is traditional in India for a great Guru to ask a disciple for an initiation fee, called *dakshina*. He might ask for anything. So Janaka asked, "What *dakshina* will you give me?" Shuka had astonishing *siddhis*, and his father was so great that even God would bow to him, so he said, "Ask for anything. I'll give you whatever you want."

"In that case," said the king, "bring me something which is of absolutely no use to anyone on the surface of the earth."

"That won't be difficult at all," said Shuka. "I can get you any number of such things." And he set out in search of something totally useless. He was a great yogi, and by the power of yoga he could travel anywhere. But no matter where he went, no matter what object he laid his hands on, he found that it had some use. When Shuka realized that he could not find anything, he felt very humiliated. He thought, "My Guru asked me to bring him just one totally useless object and I can't even do that." Very dejected and exhausted from his long search, he started back to Janaka's court. After a while, he stopped and sat under a tree to rest. When he opened his eyes, he found that someone had dropped a lump of shit next to him. He looked at it carefully, holding his nostrils. "How disgusting," he said. "This is the perfect object. Instead of going back to my Guru empty-handed, I'll take him this. It surely wouldn't be of any use to anybody." He started to pick it up, but it slipped through his hands. Again, with loathing he bent down to pick it up, and the turd began to speak.

"You piece of shit," it said, "don't touch me!"

Shuka felt as though he had melted into water. His incurable pride about his knowledge, his learning, the power of his celibacy, and his perfect self-control vanished into thin air. He was left completely humble. Still, a discriminating person always acts with discrimination, even when he finds himself in a difficult situation. So Shuka addressed the turd politely, saying, "My brother, will you kindly explain to me why you have honored me so highly by calling me a piece of shit?"

"Do you know who I am?" the turd asked.

"No, I'm afraid I don't," said Shuka.

The turd said, "Before I started hanging out with these wretched human beings, I was pizza. I was butter. I was cheese. I was displayed with great reverence in a store window. I was bought, and I was prepared with honor. But as a result of passing through a body like yours for three hours, this is what has happened to me. Now, instead of being treated as food, I am treated as shit. You have already reduced me to such a terrible condition. You'd better not touch me."

Shuka had now completely lost his conceit. He thought, "What is there about this body to be proud of?" He rushed to the king and said, "I have found the most useless object in the world."

"What is that?" asked the king.

"It is this," Shuka said, and he laid his body out flat in front of him.

"Now you are worthy of my teaching," Janaka said. He made Shuka sit close to him and said, "You have become perfect because now you are aware that the pride of the body is useless and that only Consciousness is real."

The great saint Kabir used to sing that even the body of an animal has some use. When an animal dies, its hair, its hide, and its teeth are all used in some way, but when a human being dies, absolutely nothing can be done with the body. However, if a human being were to give up his ego and go within, he would become God in an instant. Janaka transmitted a mantra and touched him, and Shuka was filled with total peace. What Shuka got from King Janaka was his own Self. He already had it, but because of his ego it had seemed to him that he did not. Shuka already had supreme love, peace, enthusiasm, and energy within him, but because of his ego, all these things had become perverted, so instead of supreme peace he was experiencing agitation, and instead of joy he was experiencing sorrow.

The moment the ego goes, all that remains is God.

2

The
Guru

The Guru Is Death

Anyone can repeat mantras, anyone can meditate, anyone can practice different kinds of *sadhana*. But the saints tell us that without the grace of the Guru none of this will bear fruit. It is only the Guru who can erase your false ego and make you realize the Self.

There are many kinds of *sadhana* for discovering the Truth. There is a big book called the *Yoga Taravali*, which explains 125,000 techniques. But if you do not have the right understanding, these techniques will only bind you. Before you begin to do *sadhana*, you are already bound. You are bound by the noose of your name, of your particular caste or stratum of society, of your idea that you belong to a particular country, of your notion that you are superior or inferior. To these you add the burden of your particular *sadhana*. You think, "I am a Christian," "I am a Sufi," "I am a hatha yogi," "I am a meditator." You are already trapped in mundane activities. You are already covered with the thick, dark ink of your caste and country and status. Then, under the pretext of erasing all these things, you simply cover yourself with the ink of a particular system. You attach the rock of a *sadhana* to your neck, and it drags you down even farther.

Sheikh Nasrudin used to sit with his ear to a wall and listen there for hours. His wife watched him doing this for a long time. Finally she asked him, "What are you hearing behind that wall?"

"Why don't you try it?" said Nasrudin. He initiated her into the technique, and she too sat down and began to listen by the wall. For a whole day, from morning until evening, she sat there, and finally she said, "O my husband, I can't hear anything."

"You've only been listening for eight hours and you are complaining that you can't hear anything," said Nasrudin, "but I have been sitting for sixteen years without hearing anything and you've never heard me complain!"

This is exactly what we do. We accept a particular path and identify ourselves with it. Then, practicing that technique, we try to discover the Truth. We think, "Tomorrow I will be able to hear something," so we keep sitting, just like Nasrudin sitting at the wall. But it does not matter what technique we practice, because no technique or path can reveal the Truth. These meshes of sadhana, these meshes of techniques, cannot reveal the brilliance of the inner Truth. How can a pot, which is inert, illumine the sun, which has thousands of effulgent rays? The sun can illumine the pot, but the pot cannot illumine the sun. In the same way, no sadhana can illumine the inner Truth, because it is that Truth which illumines all sadhana. Only if the Self reveals itself to us can we see it. And the Self reveals itself most easily through the grace of the Guru.

It is for this reason that the sages of all traditions tell us that in order to attain the Truth we need a Guru. You cannot attain the Truth through your own effort alone. If anyone is defeated by his own ego and thinks that he can do it on his own, then I can tell him that he is wasting his time. I spent forty years of my life wandering, thinking I would attain the Truth by myself. In those days I would not listen to anyone. I visited many sadhus and saints, but no matter which sadhu I went to, I would find at least one fault in him. No matter which great being I met, I would always think that I was cleverer than he. Later I realized that I was superimposing my own faults onto others and seeing my own reflection in them. I met many great saints—at least sixty of them. They would advise me, "You are a young man, you have a young body, and you should not waste your time roaming around like this." However, I would point out to them all the different faults of the different places and the different saints. Just as Shukamuni kept finding faults in Janaka, I kept finding faults in all the saints I met. Because I was like this, even though I met so many saints, I remained in the same condition that I had been in before meeting them. Because I had so much pride of knowledge, because I had so much pride in all the different types of sadhana I had performed, I was never able to even come close to the Truth. Only after forty years, when I met my Guru and

began to listen to him, did I attain something. When Shukamuni
went to Janaka he was perfect in meditation, in yoga, and in
renunciation, but because he had the pride of these things, he had
remained incomplete, unable to know the Self. It was only after
Janaka performed surgery on his ego, only when he burned the
pride he had in his body and his intellect and his various attainments,
that Shuka was able to see the Truth. In the same way, it was only
after my Guru had worked on my ego that I was able to reach my
goal.

This is the main function of the Guru: to destroy the ego of the
disciple. The Guru is death to the ego. No matter which scripture
you read, you will find that all the Guru does is to kill the ego of
the disciple. It is not that the Guru makes the disciple attain the
Self; the disciple has already attained the Self. The Guru's job is to
clean away the dirt that has accumulated around the heart—the
dirt of "I am a man," "I am the doer," "I am the giver," "I am this,"
"I am that," "I know this," and "I will do that." He burns to ashes
the disciple's limited individuality and makes him realize that he is
nothing but the supreme Lord. He frees him from the meshes of
different types of *sadhana* and makes him realize the Truth.

A Maharashtran saint put it very beautifully. He sang:

> When I was sleeping, my Guru did not give me sleeping pills so
> that I would sleep more at his door.
> Instead, he woke me from my sleep.
> I was sleeping in the delusion of ego, thinking, "I have my family, I
> have my work, I am the giver, I am the doer."
> When I woke up, I saw that there was no world, there were no men
> or women, there were no insentient objects in this universe.
> Everything was the play of God.

This is the understanding the Guru gives us, and to give us this
understanding is the Guru's function. The Guru is a being who is
saturated with the divine grace of God and who transmits it to
others. In Shaivism, it is said that God performs five actions. He
creates the universe, He sustains it, He dissolves it, and He conceals
it within His own being in order to create it again. He also bestows
His grace on suffering individual souls, so that they can realize their
oneness with Him and become free of bondage. The bestowal of
grace is the fifth action of God, and that grace-bestowing power,

that Shakti, is the Guru. The *Shiva Sutra Vimarshini* says, "The Guru is the grace-bestowing power of God." The Guru is not a body made of flesh and blood. The Guru is not a man or a woman. The Guru is not an individual being. He is the embodiment of God's power, the power of the Self. It is not a particular individual who is the Guru, but the power, the Shakti, that flows through that individual. Such a Guru has the ability to transmit God's energy into others, to awaken their own divine inner power. When this power awakens and unfolds in someone, yoga takes place on its own. Spiritual attainment happens on its own. By awakening this inner power, the Guru removes the cataracts of ignorance and ego that cover our eyes and prevent us from seeing God. Then, individuality is changed into Godhood.

The poet-saint Sunderdas said, "There is no knowledge without the Guru, no meditation without the Guru, no discipline without the Guru, no love without the Guru. Without the Guru you cannot even think about the Self. Your intellect is not illumined, nor is your delusion removed. Even the Vedas say that without the Guru you cannot attain the highest state." Therefore, it is essential to attain the grace of the Guru. No matter how many lectures you give, no matter how many things you can do, no matter how many types of *sadhana* you pursue, none of it helps you. Only when you attain the grace of such a great being do you attain something.

Although the Guru has great gifts to give us, he can give them to us only when we become worthy of receiving them. I can tell you this from my own experience. When I was a child, I met my Guru many times. We lived very close to each other, and he often used to come to my school. Along with the other children, I would climb all over him and embrace him. I was closer to him as a child than I ever was as an adult. But even though I was so close to him I did not change within; I remained as I was. After that, I wandered all over India for many years. Finally, a saint said to me, "O Muktananda Swami, go to Ganeshpuri, to Nityananda. You'll find something there." So I went to see Nityananda. But even after meeting him I did not remain with him. For several years I kept coming and going from my Baba's place. When I was there, I would become restless, so I would leave and go somewhere else for a while. The reason for this was ego and pride. Nityananda was a being who loved to insult others, and I was a person who was too proud. At his place people used to line up waiting for hours to receive something from him. He was always established in the supreme state. Sometimes he would return to the normal state of awareness in a particular mood, pick up something, call somebody close to him, and give him that. Whatever *prasad* he gave people was like a wish-fulfilling tree that would fulfill all their desires. I waited to see if I would receive anything. Nothing—not even a glass of water. Sometimes he would pick up something and say, "Come here," and I would go running. Then he would say, "Not you. I'm calling somebody else." In that way, he would insult me in front of everybody again and again, and I would die. The bigger my ego was, the worse the insults became. This went on for several years. He kept working on me, and I kept coming and going. I would leave, but then I would miss him and come back. He would work on me some more and I would leave. Finally, after a long time, he gave me something, and through his grace I attained what I had been seeking. But it was only after I had become a disciple that I was able to receive his gift.

We cannot attain the full grace of the Guru unless we become disciples. The great saint Brahmananda said, "Become the ash of the Guru's feet and then you will meet God." We have to allow the Guru to work on us, we have to dissolve our ego and pride at his feet. We may adopt a particular Guru and keep his picture on our wall and feel something when we look at it. We may have certain experiences when we meet that Guru. But if we want to be totally transformed, if we want our heart to be washed of all the filth that has accumulated there, if we want to attain everything the Guru has to give, we have to offer ourselves to the Guru without reservation. This is what it means to become a disciple. Just as you give a piece of clothing to a launderer and let him do whatever has to be done, you have to give yourself to the Guru completely and permit him to remold and reshape you in whatever way he likes.

What does giving yourself to the Guru mean? It does not mean having to stay very close to him or having to give him all your money or having to leave your family and your job and follow him wherever he goes. Nor does it mean becoming small and wretched, expecting someone to take care of you. To give yourself to the Guru means to constantly try to imbibe the Guru's instructions. Jnaneshwar Maharaj said that a true disciple is one who washes his mind in the Guru's words. He holds the Guru's knowledge in his heart, identifies himself with the Guru, and remains immersed in the Guru with the awareness that the Guru is his own inner Self. He surrenders to the Guru his sense of limitation. He merges his smallness into the Guru's vastness. Only this is the true discipleship, and a person who becomes a disciple like this does not remain stuck in discipleship. He does not become small and weak; he does not become a mere slave. Instead, he becomes established in the state the Guru has attained. By surrendering to the Guru, he himself becomes the Guru.

A disciple is one who says, like Arjuna to Lord Krishna in the *Bhagavad Gita,* "I will do Thy bidding." If the Guru commands him to do something, he follows that command scrupulously, without any doubts. Of course, it is not easy to become a disciple like this. We are used to being independent. We have our own ideas about freedom, and we are used to having our own way in everything. Then, when we come to the Guru, we see him as a human being like ourselves and project our own good and bad qualities onto him. This makes it very difficult for us to trust him. Yet to doubt the Guru or feel suspicious of him is simply to prolong our *sadhana.* The Guru will never give you a command in order to make use of you for his own purpose. The Guru will give you a command only to transform your life, to make something happen in your life. The Guru knows exactly what the disciple needs, and he will tell him to do only what is good for him.

Obedience to the Guru is the surest path to attainment. One afternoon, a group of people went to the great Siddha Kabir for *satsang.* Kabir was a weaver, and as he passed his shuttle back and forth over the loom he would chant "*Ram, Ram, Ram.*" In this way, just while weaving cloth, he had attained liberation. On that particular day, he was weaving as usual, and many people were sitting around him. Someone asked, "O Kabir, how does one attain enlightenment?" Kabir just went on weaving. After a few minutes, his shuttle fell. He called his disciple Kamal and said, "O Kamal, bring a big lantern. My shuttle has fallen on the floor." Everybody in the room was puzzled. It was mid-afternoon, and the sun was shining brightly. Why did Kabir need a lantern? Kamal brought the light and found the shuttle, which was right next to Kabir's foot. Again Kabir began to weave. Some time passed. Then the person who had asked the question spoke again: "Kabir, you haven't yet told us how to attain enlightenment." Kabir still did not reply.

Instead, he called Kamal again and said, "So many people are here. We have to give them something to eat." In India, we make a sweet dish called *kava* by boiling milk for a long time and mixing it with sugar. Kabir said, "Go and make *kava*. Put plenty of salt in it and distribute it to everybody." Kamal made the *kava* with a lot of salt, mixed it very well, and distributed it. Everyone ate it, though it tasted very salty. Kabir just kept weaving and repeating his mantra *Ram*. After a while the same person said, "O Kabir, my question is still unanswered."

"What makes you think that your question has not been answered?" Kabir asked. "Did you see Kamal? Do you think he doesn't know that when it is broad daylight you don't need a lamp to look for a shuttle? Do you think that Kamal isn't intelligent enough to have given me the shuttle without bringing the lantern to look for it? Do you think he doesn't understand that *kava* is made with sugar and not salt? When I said, 'Put salt in the *kava*,' he could have thought, 'Kabir is so old; he doesn't know what he is doing. I can put sugar in and give it to these people.' Instead, he just did what I told him to do. This is how one attains enlightenment. When a person serves his Guru like this, enlightenment comes looking for him."

Discipleship is a great and mysterious yoga. Jnaneshwar said, "All scriptures arise from one who serves the Guru's feet." The path of discipleship is the surest and easiest path to the Truth. Just by serving the Guru, just by worshipping the Guru, just by loving the Guru, a disciple attains all the Guru's knowledge. There are countless types of *sadhana* that rely on effort alone, countless paths that require a person to practice mantras and meditation techniques. But in none of these paths is it guaranteed that the goal will be reached. However, the path of the Guru is a direct path, because when a disciple surrenders himself to the Guru, the Guru takes full responsibility for his progress. The Guru guarantees that he will lead the disciple to the goal.

During Eknath Maharaj's time, there was a poor brahmin woman who had a young son named Gavba. One day the woman told Eknath that she could do nothing with the boy, and asked Eknath to take charge of him. Eknath asked the boy, "Will you stay with me if I give you *puranpolis* every day?" *Puranpolis* are a kind of sweet *chapati*. The boy was very fond of sweets, so he agreed.

He came to live with Eknath, and just as he had promised, Eknath fed him *puranpolis* every day. Because the boy loved *puranpolis* so much, people began to call him Puranpolya. He never learned anything, and his behavior was so foolish that people thought he was crazy. But he loved Eknath. Eknath was his worship. Eknath was his contemplation. Eknath was his object of study.

Several years passed, and finally the time came for Eknath to take *mahasamadhi*. Everyone realized that one of his most important works, the *Bhavartha Ramayana*, would remain incomplete if he passed away. A little while before he left his body, Eknath informed the devotees that the work would be completed by Puranpolya. The devotees were shocked. How could this illiterate boy complete Eknath's great commentary? Then, Eknath placed his hand on Puranpolya's head. From that time on, Puranpolya was an inspired being. The verses he composed were indistinguishable from his Guru's. By one touch, Eknath had transformed Puranpolya's consciousness and raised him to his own level.

This is the mystery of discipleship. When a disciple truly loses himself in the Guru, when a disciple truly surrenders himself to the Guru, he does not have to do any other spiritual practices, because the Guru's knowledge arises within him on its own. As a person serves the Guru, all supernatural powers walk around him with folded hands, and Saraswati, the goddess of knowledge, comes and sits on his tongue.

All attainments come from obeying the Guru. I can tell you this from my own experience. When I went to stay with my Guru Nityananda, he told me to go and sit in the place where Gurudev Siddha Peeth now exists. I didn't ask my Guru, "What should I do there? What should I eat?" All that I did was sit there. Some people used to bring bread once a week from Bombay. I would keep that bread for eight days, and that was what I would eat. I used to visit Nityananda Baba every day. At his place there were piles of food; so much that it would just sit there and rot. But I never asked for anything. I just obeyed his command. The result is that I received the most divine *shaktipat*. And now, even though I don't know English, I have been able to do a lot of work all over the world. Ordinarily a saint can give *shaktipat* to only two people in a week. If he transmits his energy to more than two people, he will become very weak. Not only that, a saint ordinarily can give *shaktipat* only after purifying the seeker for at least one year. He has to make the seeker do many different kinds of practices. But I have not had to follow all these rules. I have been able to give *shaktipat* to anyone who has come to me, knowing that whatever my Guru wants to make happen will happen. It is because I have surrendered completely to my Guru that I have been able to transmit Shakti to so many people all over the world. This is the power of Guru's grace; this is what you attain by following the Guru's path.

A great saint describes in one of his poems the state the Guru gives us:

> *When I met that pure One, I also became pure.*
> *From him I received grace, and after that I began to meditate.*
> *As I meditated, my individuality vanished,*
> *And I myself became Consciousness.*
> *I myself became the Guru....*
>
> *When my inner ego was struck by the sword of my Guru's love,*
> *That love began to kill my ego,*
> *So that even though I was alive, I experienced death.*
> *My death died, and I became immortal.*
> *When I received the Guru's touch, he took away my sleep of delusion.*
> *The fire of knowledge was kindled in me,*
> *And it burned up all my involvements.*
> *It burned away my bondage and I became completely free.*
> *When I met the Pure, when I merged into the Pure, I also*
>   *became pure.*
> *When I met that ecstatic being, my individuality vanished,*
> *And I became God.*

Living with the Guru

Q: Is it necessary for disciples to live with the Guru closely for a long time in order to get the most from their association with him?

SM: It is not necessary to live with the Guru. What is necessary is that you have love for the Guru and that you have interest in the Truth. A person who is not established in his *sadhana* may stay very close to the Guru, but he is still far away from the Guru. It is not enough merely to be with the Guru if you do not follow the Guru's path. If you live close to the Guru but remain far away from *sadhana*, you will not attain much.

When Nityananda Baba was in this world, there was a boy with him called Rodkya. Nityananda loved that boy very much, and other people also gave him a lot of respect. Baba used to receive different kinds of food and cloth, and Rodkya was the main distributor of those things. He would eat very good food, and he became very healthy and strong and puffed up. Then he grew up and became fifteen. There was a river close by, and every day he would go fishing. When Baba wanted Rodkya, he would call him, and people would say, "O Baba, he has gone fishing." If a person does not have discipline, if he does not know the greatness of *sadhana*, if he is not pure, then no matter where he is and no matter what he does it is worthless. The boy would sleep right next to Nityananda Baba, but all that he did was go fishing. Now he is a florist; he sells garlands and lives on whatever he gets from that.

No matter where you live, you should have self-control and you should be engaged in *sadhana*. You should lose yourself completely in devotion. Only then will you benefit from everything. If a person is not seeking That, then even if he is staying with the Guru he does not really benefit from the Guru. He appears to be living with the Guru, but he actually lives with somebody else.

If you live with the Guru having the desire for liberation, you will progress very quickly. But if you fully understand the Guru, you can never be away from him. Your inner Self is God, and it is also the Guru. A saint said, "Consciousness, God, the Guru, the Shakti live right in your body." The inner Self is always within you, so how can you ever be away from the Guru? Someone asked Rabi'a, "O Rabi'a, where does your Guru live?"

"He lives with me," she replied.

"How can that be?"

"The knowledge my Guru has given to me and the mantra my Guru has given to me are with me in this very body. That is why he lives with me."

A true Guru stays with you; no matter where his physical body is, he does not live far away from you. A Guru is not a mere individual body; he is not an individual being. The Guru is divine Shakti. He is called a Guru who transmits his own Shakti into a disciple so that it permeates every pore of his body. When a disciple receives *shaktipat* initiation from a Guru, he is given a mantra. The Guru is one with that mantra, and in the form of the mantra he enters the disciple. So how can you say that the Guru is far away from you? He is constantly within you, and his energy permeates every pore and blood cell of your body. He is very close to you.

A Personal Relationship

Q: The people who spend a lot of time with you seem to get lots of personal teaching and work on their egos. How can people who do not have a personal relationship with you get the benefit of that teaching?

SM: A person should not try to have a personal relationship in order to get the benefit of someone's teachings. The Lord of all beings dwells within everyone's heart. You should meditate on Him and remember Him. Then you will attain what you are supposed to attain. It will come of its own accord without your trying to attain it. Nowadays you can get these teachings wherever you want to. There are many shops for teachings. You do not lack them. To realize the Self, only two words are enough. You do not have to study a lot. You do not have to read many books. Nor do you have to put forth a lot of your own effort. If you can imbibe only two words, they will be more than enough to enable you to cross the ocean of the world. When you have an intense longing to attain That, when you are thirsty to attain that supreme Truth, then this Truth reveals itself in your own heart. Where is that place where there is no Self? Who is there who does not have this Self? The scriptures say, "God is apparent." So how can you say that you cannot see the Self which dwells everywhere and in your own heart? Why do you have to put forth a lot of effort to attain what already exists within you? The thing is, you should have intense longing to attain That, and you should also be filled with tender devotion.

A Guru Has His Own Ways

You should follow the path taught by the Guru, not imitate his ways. If you simply imitate him, there is a danger that you will fall.

It is for this reason that many students of Siddhas become bound.

I read a story about the saint Makarios. He was a great Siddha, a fully realized being. Since he was always immersed in ecstasy, many people began to follow him and spend time with him. They would imitate the Guru's outer ways without paying any attention to his inner state, his inner teaching. One day Makarios was sitting with his disciples on the shore of a lake. While Makarios was lecturing to his students, he put his hand into the water, took out a few fish, and swallowed them alive. The Guru had swallowed only three or four small fish, but when the disciples saw the Guru do this, they set upon the fish and took at least thirty or forty of them. They cooked and spiced them and then ate them, feeling very happy that they were with such a wonderful Guru. After a while, the party moved on to another lake, which was much bigger. There was not a single fish in this lake. Now Makarios spat out into the lake the four fish he had swallowed. They were still alive and began to sport in the water. He said to his students, "Since you ate so many fish from the other lake, let us see if you can bring them up here." The disciples tried to spit out the fish they had eaten, but all that came up was decayed matter.

This is not what I mean when I say you should follow the Guru. A Guru has his own ways, and they are highly mysterious. You cannot know why he does the things he does, and if you simply follow them blindly, they will lead you into a pit. Instead of imitating the Guru, you should stand firmly on the path the Guru has shown. If you really want to advance on the spiritual path, you have to be very firm, very resolute, and very disciplined. If you leave yourself loose, you will fall very quickly. A disciple must also do his own work and have faith in it. Whatever your field of activity, you should stick to it and follow the teaching of the Guru along with it. You must avoid lethargy, you must be very dynamic, and as far as possible you should live by the fruit of your own labor and then follow the path shown by the Guru. This is what you should do after having found the Guru. You should keep going farther and farther ahead on the path. The ideal is to give yourself completely to the Guru and in return become the Guru yourself. Jnaneshwar Maharaj said, "I have been saved. I have been saved by the grace of my Guru. I have swum across to the other shore." This is what should happen.

The Guru's grace should not drown you. You should not become caught up in a situation where you are neither here nor there.

Mind Reading

Q: Some people say that the Guru knows everything, that he knows all your thoughts and so forth. Yet it is obvious that he does not know everything on this level of consciousness—all languages, all people, all names. When people say the Guru knows all, are they speaking of the universal Guru rather than the individual Guru?

SM: I don't know what Guru you are speaking about, the universal Guru or the individual Guru. All I know is that the Guru is certainly aware of all your thoughts and of everything else that is going on. He does not need to know all the mundane languages; just one language is enough, and that is the language in which God communicates, the language of the heart. God does not communicate in English or French or Spanish.

The Guru should not be confused with a psychic. You expect things like mind reading from a psychic. The Guru's concern is with the one Reality which is in everyone. He is not concerned with which particular disease an individual may suffer from. The Guru takes pleasure only in the Consciousness within seekers, not the garbage in their minds. To a Guru, the thoughts and fancies which keep arising in the mind are mere trash. He transcends the mind and lives continually in the state beyond the mind. Why should he be conscious of what is in others' minds when he has risen above his own mind? If he is not interested in what is happening in his own mind, why should he plunge into the hell of another's mind? Suppose that there is a person who is thinking negatively about someone else. Should the Guru become aware of that? A Guru likes to be aware only of the supreme Truth; he delights only in that. So why should he be aware of all the thoughts in another's mind?

An event occurred in India involving a royal guru and a Siddha Guru. The royal guru was sitting in meditation under a tree when all of a sudden his mind was distracted by the thought of the prince's coronation. He was wondering what kind of horse the prince should ride in the coronation procession and exactly how it should be decorated. Just then the Siddha Guru appeared. The royal guru was very proud of the fact that he was the guru of the king, while the Siddha Guru was totally free of pride and was immersed in his inner ecstasy.

There are two things that drive a person to ask a question: fear and the desire to test. This royal guru asked the Siddha, "Do you know what thoughts are in my mind?"

The Siddha replied, "Why should one who is reveling in the kingdom of God take interest in decorating a horse?"

Why should a saint take any interest in the filth of anybody's mind?

What the Guru Asks

Q: A disciple asks much of his Guru. What in turn does a Guru ask of his disciple?

SM: A true Guru wants nothing from a disciple. Is the Guru a perfect being or an imperfect being? If he is a perfect being, he will not want anything from anyone. In the ancient times, Gurus used to live in forest hermitages, and their needs were extremely few. Disciples would come and serve at the ashram, but that was not so much for the Guru's sake as for their own growth. The Indian scriptures say that a disciple should give whatever he has to a Guru, but the Guru must not accept anything from a disciple except his ignorance.

Surrender

Q: What does it mean to surrender the fruit of one's actions to the Guru?

SM: The *Bhagavad Gita* says that to surrender all the fruit of all one's actions is a great practice. Even to do actions without desire for their fruit is a great practice. Surrendering all your actions to God means that if you listen to something, you listen for God. If you eat some food, you eat for God. If you live in this world, you do that for God too. Whatever you do is for God. The truth is that even if a person thinks that he does something, it is really God who does everything and God who experiences everything. There is a scripture in Shaivism which says that it is God who breathes and God who hears, God who gives and God who takes. If a person leads his life with awareness, then his life becomes great and he attains the happiness of God. The only obstacle in the way of attaining God's happiness is the sense of "I"-ness. When you iden-tify yourself with that "I," you become the slave of your senses. When you tie a dog to a leash, you can take the dog anywhere; it is under your control. In the same way, when you identify yourself with the ego, with the "I"-ness, you are controlled by your senses, and the senses make you do whatever they want you to do. That is why it is so good, no matter what actions you perform, to surrender those actions to God. A person who has surrendered in this way lives completely without anxiety.

Once King Janaka asked his Guru, Yajnavalkya, "When will I attain the highest Reality?"

Yajnavalkya replied, "The moment you surrender yourself in body, mind, and material wealth, you will attain Him."

"All I want is peace," Janaka said, "so I give you everything."

Yajnavalkya said, "If you have given everything to me, then you will certainly get peace."

The next day everyone assembled for a spiritual discussion, and while it was going on, a brahmin priest appeared. He went to Janaka and said, "I have to perform the sacred thread ceremony for my son but I have no money. Please give me some." At first, the priest made his request in a courteous and correct manner. However, the king remained silent. When the priest saw that he was not getting any response from the king, he began to swear at him. He said, "You wicked creature. You do not even know how to look after your own subjects! I will place a curse on you!" But the king still did not react. When the brahmin finally became tired of swearing at the king and went away, the people who were present said, "O your Majesty, you are such a great person, and that man swore at you in such a flagrant manner. Why didn't you take action against him?"

The king replied, "I do not have anything with which to react to the swear words he showered on me because I have given everything to the Guru. Along with my body, I gave him my wealth, so I did not have a single penny to give the brahmin. I also gave my mind away, so now I have nothing to worry with or about."

Yajnavalkya said, "If this is your attitude, you have truly given everything!"

When you have truly surrendered everything, you are not attached to anything. If you surrender the fruit of your actions, you receive the greatest fruit.

The Meaning of Surrender

Q: Do trust and surrender arise by themselves or can I will them?

SM: You have to create the feeling of trust inside. However, when understanding arises, surrender takes place of its own accord. You do not have to do anything. Many people ask me to explain surrender. However, they do not have the right understanding. When you do not understand the meaning of surrender, the secret of surrender, you do not feel like surrendering. If there is a gutter full of filthy water and the water runs into the sacred water of the Ganga, that gutter water also becomes sacred water. All its impurities and filth disappear. However, if the gutter is very much attached to its filth, if it is afraid of losing its filth, it might not like the idea of surrendering itself to the Ganga.

What does anyone really lose through surrender except his impurities and negativities? We are afraid of surrender because we do not understand its secret. Most people confuse surrender with slavery, and that is why they are afraid of it. Surrender is not slavery. In fact, surrender frees you from slavery and brings you total freedom. True surrender is having the awareness of God in everything, in every feeling, action, and vision. Wherever you look you should see the pulsation of Consciousness. You should experience the inspiration of Consciousness. That is true surrender.

Serving the Guru

Q: How can a devotee best serve the Guru? I have a family, a job, and many responsibilities, and I want to do your work.

SM: You have very few responsibilities, and only one family. There have been so many people who have many families; still they do this work. Janaka was a great king, a great sovereign; still he did this work. Man can offer his *seva*, his selfless service, to the Guru at any time. The true *seva*, the inner *seva*, is this: Always concentrate on *So'ham*. Try to increase the space between *so* and *ham* and become established in that space. That is true *guruseva*. You can also offer your outer service whenever you have time and whenever it is convenient for you. You can offer your service in many, many different ways. You can speak to one or two other people about what you have experienced, what you have received. If you were to tell two or four people in your office or in your working field that such a state exists, even that would be a great *seva*. However, the greatest *seva* is to become completely anchored in *Purno'ham*, in the perfect "I"-consciousness — to become completely still every moment in the space between the two syllables. You should become still in between the two syllables, and there should not be any movement. Now this should happen naturally. Don't try to do it. In India there is a saying: "A man wanted to make a pipe to smoke, but he ended up making a big bucket." Don't do that. As the *prana* goes out and comes in naturally, try to get into the space between the two syllables. That is a great state. If you look at the pictures of the great beings with this awareness, you will know they have become established in *aham*. *Ham* turns into *Purno'ham*.

So this is a great *seva*. Ordinary *seva* — sweeping the floor, giving money, giving food, giving clothes, pots, and pans — is all right too, if you want to do it also. You do this ordinary *seva* because you think it is your duty. You think that is the true understanding, but true *guruseva* is to get hold of that space and try to increase its duration. The Guru has told you to do this, and this is the true *guruseva*. You should carry it out completely.

Service to the Guru is a great mystery. Once there was a Guru who had two disciples. He told them that That was all-pervasive, that you could hear it from anywhere, that you could speak to it from anywhere, that you could see it anywhere, and that if you would put your hand out, it would grab your hand. One day the Guru called both of his disciples and gave them a sweet called *balushai*. It was really delicious, and they could smell its aroma. He told each of them to find a place where there was nobody else, and to eat the sweet there. One of the disciples just stood there in the awareness of nonwisdom; all he wanted to do was to eat the *balushai*. Eventually he went outside, hid behind a pillar, and swallowed it. Then he returned to the classroom, feeling very pleased with himself. The other disciple set off in search of a place where there was nobody else and was gone a long, long time. Finally, he returned. When both disciples were together again, the Guru met them and asked, "Did you eat the *balushai*?"

The first disciple said, "Yes, Guruji, I ate it two days ago. I was the first one to eat it."

"Where did you eat it?"

"Do you see that bridge over there? Behind the bridge there is a pillar and I hid behind the pillar and ate it."

The Guru asked the other disciple, "What about you?"

The second disciple gave the *balushai* back to the Guru. He had not eaten it.

The Guru said, "He ate his two days ago, within a second. Why have you not eaten yours?"

The disciple said, "I wanted to eat it, but everywhere I went I would remember your teaching that That exists everywhere, that it is all-pervasive. No matter where I went, I felt its presence. There was no place where there was nobody else."

The Guru said, "You have passed." The one who ate the *balushai* passed in eating, and the one who did not eat it passed in knowledge and in wisdom. When you pass in this way, when you become established in the words of the Guru, you are performing true *seva*.

The Perfect Disciple

Q: You tell us that the perfect disciple is one who obeys his Guru without question, like the disciple who puts salt in the sweet pudding because his Guru tells him to. But how do we know what to do when the Guru does not tell us physically or when the Guru says something but we feel he may really mean something else?

SM: If a person has a clean and pure heart, he will know spontaneously what the Guru wants without having to ask him. Once my

Baba told me not to eat mangoes. I did not ask my Baba whether he meant that I should not eat mangoes for a week or for a month. For twelve years I did not eat mangoes. In India, mangoes are considered to be the best fruit. I did all my *sadhana* under a mango tree; you may have seen a photo of me sitting on that tree like a monkey. Under that mango tree I saw something. I found something. After twelve years my Baba gave me a mango to eat, and I began to eat mangoes once again. I found them very sweet.

It is very difficult for a disciple to be perfectly obedient and to become a perfect disciple. Kabir says, "If you take a small pot, no matter where you go to fill it—whether to a water faucet, to a well, to a river, or to an ocean—you can fill the pot only to its brim. You cannot fill it past its limited capacity." It is very difficult to become a perfect disciple like Kamal. Nonetheless, you can lead a pure life and pursue your mundane activities. If you cannot become a perfect disciple, at least become an imperfect disciple.

Dependence

Q: Yesterday you said something about depending on the Guru. I have very rarely depended on others, because I have not found many people on whom I could depend. You seem to be pretty dependable, but I still find it hard to depend on you. Do you have any suggestions on how I should solve this problem?

SM: By depending on the Guru I mean that you should depend on him for help and support. Having the faith that the Guru will certainly give you Shakti, that he will always protect you, is what I mean by depending on the Guru. In the *Bhagavad Gita* great stress is laid on dependence on God. Lord Krishna tells Arjuna, "Take refuge in Me alone. Give yourself completely to Me, and I will free you from all evils." If a sick person hands himself over to a doctor's care, he has faith that the doctor will try every possible means within his power to cure him. A baby depends on his mother completely and has faith that she will look after him in every possible way. Similarly, you should learn to depend on the Guru with the faith that you will certainly receive something from him. This is devotion of a very high order. Such devotion brings meditation.

Ruthlessness and Compassion

Q: Why have the Gurus of history often seemed to behave so ruthlessly toward their disciples? What is the relationship between the Guru's ruthlessness and his compassion?

SM: The Guru's ruthlessness is his compassion. I read a poem by Kabir Sahib. He said that the Guru is like a potter. A potter shapes a pot by giving it blows from the outside with one of his hands, but at the same time he supports it from within with his other hand so that it will not collapse. In the same way, on the outside a Guru may seem to be beating up a disciple, but on the inside he is always supporting and protecting him. So the Guru is ruthless, and he is also very compassionate.

I read a story by Sheikh Sadi, who was a great being. Once there was a teacher who disciplined his students by shaking a stick at them. One day a *sadhu* came to the school. He went inside, and all the children were making a lot of noise. The teacher scolded the children. Immediately they stopped making noise and sat very quietly. The *sadhu* did not like what he saw; he said, "It is not good to discipline children so strictly, because then they do not grow." This is what people say in Western countries. The *sadhu* told all the heads of the other schools in the district that this teacher was much too strict and that they should do something about it. From then on, the teacher became very loose. He did not care about his students; all he wanted was his salary. In two years the *sadhu* returned. He saw that the children were not even in the classroom. Instead, they were all playing and fighting outside. They were not learning anything. Sheikh Sadi drew his own conclusion. He said, "A teacher's beating is sweeter than the parents' delicious food."

So there is compassion in the Guru's ruthlessness. The Guru is neither a violent person nor a being who wants to get up a party among his disciples. To eliminate the faults and defects of his disciples, he sometimes may appear to behave in a very crude and ruthless fashion, yet in that very ruthlessness there is great tenderness and compassion.

Tulsidas says in his *Ramayana* that when there is a boil on the body of a small child, the mother does not put powder on it and fan it. She makes her heart very strong, and then she lances the boil, and throws it away. It hurts the child, and the child weeps very loudly. In the same way, because of his love for his disciple, the Guru uses the harshest method, the crudest method, to eliminate his shortcomings. Even if the disciple is weeping bitterly, even if it hurts him, still he does not care.

Effort and Grace

Q: In sadhana how much is self-effort and how much is Guru's grace?

SM: If you are completely able to receive grace from the Guru, then you do not need any self-effort. Everything happens through grace. But because you lack full faith and one-pointedness, you do not receive this grace fully, and therefore you have to do sadhana. Even after practicing sadhana for a while, at the end you have to receive grace in order to attain realization.

The Guru's Curse

Q: What should a person do if the Guru forsakes or curses him?

SM: Even if the Guru forsakes the disciple, the disciple should not forsake the Guru. You must know the story of Eklavya and Dronacharya. When Eklavya approached his Guru, Dronacharya, Dronacharya did not accept him. However, Eklavya did not forsake his Guru. Thereby, he attained everything. A Guru will not curse you. If a disciple makes many, many mistakes, a Guru will tell him, "Go back to your own home." But why should a Guru curse his disciple? Gurus are bestowers of grace, and that is all that they do all the time. If there is a Guru who has the power to curse somebody, even his apparent curse turns out to be beneficial.

Once there were some sages in a place called Kishkindha, in Karnataka, a state in south India. They all believed in Shiva, and they worshipped the shivalingam. Whenever the sages went into the river to take a dip, two monkeys, Nala and Nila, would go to the bank of the river, pick up the shivalingam, and throw it into the water. Finally the sages got tired of the monkeys' mischief.

One day, one of the sages cursed them. He said, "O Nala and Nila, you are causing so much trouble! From now on, if you put anything in the water, it will never sink."

The next day, the monkeys continued their mischief. They picked up the *shivalingam* and threw it into the water, but the *lingam* did not sink. Instead, it floated on the water. It was very easy for the sages to pick it up and return it to the proper place. As it happened, their curse turned into such a great boon. Once Lord Rama, who was on a military expedition, wanted to cross the ocean very quickly and he needed to build a bridge. He took the help of Nala and Nila, because when they put huge rocks into the ocean, the rocks would float. It was very easy to build a bridge, and they accomplished the task in no time. Rama and his army walked over that bridge to the other side of the ocean.

Your question is crooked. A Guru is one with God. If God is love, is not the Guru also love? A true Guru will never try to harm anyone. If a Guru gives a curse, he is not a true Guru. Even if a Guru should ever curse you, he would do so knowing it would be for your own good, just like the sages who cursed Nala and Nila.

However, if a person had committed bad actions, if he were full of them, then even if a sage bestowed his grace on that person, still that grace would turn into a curse. In the *Ramayana* there is a dialogue between Bharadwaja and Romaharshana, who, after he was cursed, was given the name Kakabhushendi. While he was still Romaharshana, he went to Bharadwaja and asked him some questions about the knowledge of Brahman. Bharadwaja systematically explained the Truth to him. After explaining something to a student, a teacher of Vedanta usually asks, "Have you understood?" If the student answers, "No," then the teacher will explain it to him again. If the student answers, "I have understood it," then the teacher will ask, "Do you accept it?" If the answer is "No," then the teacher will explain it to the student once again so that he can accept it.

Bharadwaja was such a great sage that Lord Ramachandra, the incarnation of God, visited him. All the other sages used to visit Lord Ramachandra, but he visited Bharadwaja. Even though he explained the knowledge of the Absolute very clearly to Romaharshana four times, still Romaharshana did not accept it. He thought he was such a great sage that he could not accept the teaching. So whenever Bharadwaja asked him if he understood the Truth, he would say, "No." He insulted Bharadwaja's knowledge. Finally, Bharadwaja said, "If you refuse to believe that this is the Truth, then you are worthy of becoming a crow." At that very moment,

Romaharshana became a crow. When he turned from a human being into a crow, immediately he said, "I accept the teaching." Wouldn't it have been better if he had accepted the Truth when he was still a human being? But it was only after he became a crow that Kakabhushendi began to understand that Bharadwaja had great nectarean knowledge. Still he wondered why it was that when Bharadwaja was such a great sage, he could get angry and curse him. After Kakabhushendi had wondered about this for a long time, he received an answer from within. He realized that if two pieces of sandalwood are rubbed against each other, they emit fragrance, because sandalwood has its own quality. However, if a piece of sandalwood is rubbed against a piece of ordinary wood, then both catch fire. Kakabhushendi realized that although his Guru was full of great knowledge, he had not been sufficiently worthy to receive it; all he had been able to elicit from the Guru was the fire of anger. Then he asked Bharadwaja for forgiveness, apologizing for the arrogance and pride he had shown in not accepting his knowledge. Before he was turned into Kakabhushendi, the great sage Romaharshana had thought he was so great that he could not accept Bharadwaja's teaching. But after he became a crow, he became humble, and in time he attained the Truth. So Bharadwaja's curse was really a blessing.

Testing the Disciple

Q: When does a disciple become a Guru? How does he know that he has become perfect?

SM: A disciple becomes a Guru when he follows the *sadhana* that has been laid down by his Guru and loses himself in it. Then he attains Guruhood. A disciple who is tested and who passes the test becomes the Guru. He is the real disciple. Whoever comes to me says, "O Baba, if you are the Guru, I am your disciple." I say, "Hum, yes." Only when they are tested do I know how many of these people are real disciples. During the time of Tukaram Maharaj, there were many devotees of Hari, or God. They all had left their jobs and work. They would say, "Rama, Krishna, Hare," and would go to other people's houses to eat. That is how they led their lives.

Wherever Tukaram Maharaj was, thousands and thousands of people would gather. They would all wear a turban on their head, carry a *veena*, an Indian musical instrument, and would repeat, "*Rama, Krishna, Hare.*" In those days the devotees of Hari would go to people and spread their arms, begging for alms. In Maharashtra, half of the population had become devotees of Tukaram Maharaj, and they had all left their jobs. King Shivaji was in a predicament. He consulted his prime minister, saying, "Everyone has not become Tukaram Maharaj. No one has been tested. We have to test everyone." If there are disciples who are not tested, then it is very possible for the good heart, the good faith, and the good conduct of other disciples to be spoiled. Shivaji's prime minister came up with a means of testing Tukaram's devotees. He issued a proclamation: "On the fifteenth of January, all the devotees of Tukaram will be hanged." He told the town crier to beat the drum and make this announcement. The very next day all the Tukarams threw away their turbans and *veenas*. Only one Tukaram Maharaj was left. In the same way, only if I test them will I know how many real disciples there are.

3

Spiritual Practice

The Milk of a Lioness

When I was traveling in the West, people used to come up to me at railway stations and airports and say, "Give me mantra. Give me *shaktipat*." They must have thought I had a bundle of *shaktipat* in my pocket, and that I could produce it and give it to them like a pill. But it does not work like that. Shakti is a divine substance which is attained only when you have attained the supreme state of faith, when you have gone beyond everything, when you are bathed with virtues. You have to understand the value of the Shakti. You have to know how to take care of it. The purer you become on the inside, the more you are able to receive from the Guru, and the more clearly you are able to see the Truth.

Once a king went to a sage and beseechingly asked the sage to give him knowledge. The sage said, "Of course I will give you something; however, first you must give me something." The Guru will always ask the disciple for some offering before he initiates him. He does this not because he needs anything, but because without giving anything, the disciple cannot get anything.

"I can give you whatever you ask for," said the king.

"Then go," said the Guru, "and bring me the milk of a lioness."

It was not difficult for the king to get the milk of a lioness. After all, he was a sovereign; he had many lions and lionesses. So he took a container made of steel and got the milk and returned to the Guru. But the milk of a lioness is very strong; it eats through everything. Therefore, even before the king had reached the Guru's ashram, the milk had flowed out of the steel container. The king said, "O Babaji, the milk is gone. It ate its way through the container."

The sage said, "Go back home and get a golden container and bring the milk in that." The king went home and put the milk in a golden container. It remained in the container. "O king," said the Guru, "did you see that?"

"Yes," said the king. "The milk wouldn't stay in the steel container, but the golden one held it."

The Guru said, "Your heart is made like that. If I pour any grace in it, it will all run out. So change your heart and make it into gold. Then you will be able to receive my grace. If the heart is not strong enough, the grace just flows out."

This story has great significance. Sometimes people ask me, "Why is it that we do not experience enlightenment the moment we receive the Guru's Shakti?" I can only say that if you had enough worthiness, then it would be enough for you to hear one word from the Guru and you would be liberated. When I say that you should be worthy I do not mean that you should know how to decorate yourself very beautifully or that you should be very clever and able to understand things with your intellect. I do not mean that you should be able to push other people aside and make yourself first. I mean that your heart should be full of pure and noble feelings. The great Shankaracharya had a disciple named Hastamalaka. One day Hastamalaka met his Guru walking on the road. He asked him, "O Guruji, who am I?" Shankaracharya replied, "You are That!" Immediately, without a moment's hesitation, Hastamalaka understood the meaning of what his Guru had said and became enlightened. He was so worthy that he was able to assimilate the Guru's knowledge within a moment. If you had a heart like Hastamalaka's, it would not take you even that much time to realize the Truth. The great sage Vasishtha told Lord Rama, "The Truth is so close to you that you can know it in the time it takes to blink your eyes. Yet many ages have passed and you still have not seen it." If your heart were completely pure, if you had complete faith and were completely surrendered, you would experience the Truth immediately. But because you do not have this kind of faith, you have to do *sadhana*. You have to meditate. You have to practice mantra repetition. Only then will you be able to hold the Guru's Shakti. Only then will you be able to assimilate his teachings.

For so many years, you have been accumulating the impressions of the world. You have been filling your mind and heart with the notion that you are small, that you are weak, that you are sinful. You have learned these things from your teachers, from your society, and from the holy books of different religions, and you have come to believe them. You have thought of yourself as a limited creature, and you have learned to see sin in the pure Self. As a result you have been swimming in the ocean of limited feelings—desires and cravings, attachment and aversion, anger and jealousy. Now your mind and heart have become so foggy and dull that you cannot see the light of the Self, and even when someone tells you that you are the Self, you cannot accept it. That is why you have to do *sadhana*. *Sadhana* is the means by which you can make your heart pure enough and strong enough to hold the knowledge of the Truth.

The purer you are on the inside, the more clearly you are able to perceive the Self. When you first receive *shaktipat*, you may have an experience of That, but to hold that experience, to become established in that experience, you have to practice for a long time. Therefore, just as you eat, drink, and do your work every day, you should also practice *sadhana* in a disciplined manner. People come and take a course for two or three days and then go home and forget everything they have learned. They do not practice what they have learned. Then they think, "I took that course, I was with that Guru, but nothing has stayed with me." The truth is that only if you practice every day, only if you combine *sadhana* with your worldly activities, will the Guru's knowledge bear fruit for you. Even to attain something in daily life you have to work for it. It does not matter what field you are in, whether you are a scientist or an artist or a businessman; if you want to earn something you must work for it. When this is the case in ordinary life, why should it be different in spiritual life? Why should you expect to attain the Truth in a few days? Oil is inherent in sesame seeds, but if you just take some sesame seeds in your hand, you do not see the oil; you have to follow a process in order to extract it. Butter is contained in milk, but you have to churn the milk to get the butter. Fire is in wood, but if you simply touch a piece of wood, the fire will not burn your hand; you have to rub two pieces of wood together before the fire is produced. In the same way, even though the Self is fully manifest within us, it is only through the awakening of the Shakti and the process of *sadhana* that it is revealed.

You may feel that it would be very good if the goal of *sadhana* were to come to you effortlessly. Today many workers have the same attitude. They feel that their employers should work hard and that they should get the bonuses. Similarly, many students want their professors to study while they get the degrees. Many of my devotees also say, "Baba, give me your grace and let everything happen inside me." In this way, they are behaving like Sheikh Nasrudin.

One evening Nasrudin had had too much to drink. He was lying on the sidewalk, completely intoxicated. A policeman approached him, shook him and said, "Hey, brother, it's midnight. You should get up and go home."

Nasrudin said, "I don't have to get up. The entire town is spinning around me. As soon as my house comes around, I'll just go inside!"

It would be wonderful if the destination of *sadhana* came to you like that, but unfortunately things do not work this way. To attain the Self you have to meditate on the Self. If your *sadhana* is not pure and strong, then even if God reveals Himself to you, you will not be able to see Him. All you will see is a vision; you will not understand that it is God. When Lord Rama and Lord Krishna were in this world, millions of people saw them, but not all these people were liberated. For this reason, your *sadhana* should be high. While doing *sadhana*, you should have one goal: to establish a relationship between yourself and God. Your *sadhana* should be internal, not external—the best *sadhana* is the natural meditation that arises after the awakening of the inner Shakti. Your *sadhana* should also be persistent. You should meditate and meditate; you should meditate so much that the vibrations of meditation begin to flow in every part of your body. At one time, I was afflicted with chronic malaria. I had the germs of malaria within me, and for that reason the disease kept returning. In the same way, your *sadhana*, your meditation, your mantra repetition, and your remembrance of the Self should become chronic for you. No matter what circumstance you are in, these things should never leave you.

When Mahatma Gandhi was shot, he did not scream or wail, nor did he cry for help. The only words that came out of his mouth were "Hey, Rama." He was shot four times, and four times he called, "Hey, Rama." He had repeated the name of Rama his entire life, and the name had permeated his blood. For this reason, even in calamity, all that he said was "Rama."

Your knowledge and your *sadhana* should be like that. They should be such that they come to help you at the right time. When you get angry, forgiveness should arise within you so that you can subdue your anger. When greed arises, moderation should come and stand before you so that you can defeat your greed. When a desire comes up, detachment should stand before you so that it can eradicate your desire. Whatever you study, whatever you practice should be written in your blood so that no one can erase it.

The fact is that as you constantly meditate, as you become absorbed in the remembrance of the Self in all, the experience of the Self will begin to flow out through all your gestures and looks. Your *sadhana* will pervade every pore and blood cell in your body. Then you will not have to make an effort to do *sadhana*, because the vibrations of *sadhana* in your body will force you to do *sadhana*.

I'll tell you a true story. Eknath Maharaj was a great Siddha of Maharashtra who wrote a beautiful commentary on the *Shrimad Bhagavatam*. Every day, Eknath used to read stories from the *Bhagavatam*. All the people of the town would come and listen, except for one man. He was a landlord named Kulkarni. One day Eknath went to see the landlord. "Everyone comes to hear the stories of the *Bhagavatam* except you," he said. "Why don't you come?"

"Oh, Maharaj," the landlord replied, "you don't understand how busy I am. I have property in seven towns!"

"Of what use will your seven towns be to you at the time of your death?" Eknath asked. Eknath was a great Siddha, and the force of his words pierced the landlord's heart.

"What should I do?" he asked.

"Is there any time in the day when you are free?" asked Eknath.

"There is no time at all," the man said.

"You take a bath every day, don't you?" asked Eknath.

"Of course," said the man. In India, everyone goes to the river every morning to bathe. That is the custom.

"Every day, as you are pouring water during your bath, recite these five mantras from the *Bhagavatam*. That will be enough."

The landlord agreed to do this. From that time on, every day as he poured water over himself, he would recite these mantras. Years passed, and at last he died. His people laid out the body and, as is the custom in India, gave it a bath. The moment they began pouring water over the body, it sprang up and began to repeat the mantras.

This man had received the grace of a great Siddha, and he had practiced the same mantras one-pointedly for many years. The result was that they had come to permeate his body totally, so that they repeated themselves automatically. If this was the case with this man, who did only one small practice, think how it must be for someone who permeates his life with *sadhana*.

Tukaram Maharaj was also a great Siddha of Maharashtra. He lived as a householder in a small village called Dehu. His *sadhana* was to repeat the name of the Lord. He would constantly repeat, "Vitthale, Vitthale, Vitthale," and would experience the presence of Vitthal in everything.

The essence of *sadhana* is the constant remembrance of the goal of *sadhana*, the Self. When you meditate, you should meditate on the Self. When you repeat the mantra, you should do it with the awareness that the mantra is one with the Self. When you do your work, you should do it with the Self in mind. When you are talking to someone, you should have the Self in front of your eyes. Whatever you do, wherever you go, wherever you look, you should have the awareness that the Self is there. To understand the presence of the Self everywhere, to feel the presence of the Self everywhere, to meditate with the awareness that the Self is everywhere—this is *sadhana*, and this is how Tukaram Maharaj lived his life. After a while, as a result of his practice, great scriptures began to arise from within him. He became an omniscient being who was able to see the past, present, and future. It was the power of God's name that gave him the ability to do all these things. As he repeated "Vitthale, Vitthale, Vitthale," he attained a state in which he saw only God in everything and in which he was totally under the control of the Supreme.

In those days, when a person had to go to the toilet he would take a bowl of water and go off far away from his house into the forest. One day Tukaram took his bowl of water and began to walk. He was so focused on Vitthal that he continued to repeat the name even as he walked. When people heard him they were shocked. Orthodox Hindus follow certain rituals in everything they do. According to orthodox Hinduism, excreting waste matter is an impure action, so a person is not supposed to repeat the Lord's name while he does it. These orthodox people followed Tukaram and saw that when he sat down to excrete he kept repeating "Vitthale, Vitthale."

They began to harass him, saying, "Why are you repeating the Name in such a place?"

"I'm sorry," said Tukaram, "but my speech is not under my control. I can't help myself."

"We'll see about that," said the people. They took a piece of cloth and wound it around Tukaram's mouth. "Now let's see if you keep repeating the name of Vitthal!" Suddenly, they heard the name of Vitthal coming out of every pore of Tukaram's body. Before, he had been saying the Name only with his mouth, but now it was thundering out of every pore.

This is what the fruit *sadhana* should be. But *sadhana* bears this kind of fruit only when you practice it constantly, for a long time, and with the right understanding. The sage Vasishtha said that there are two aspects of *sadhana*, meditation and understanding, and that only when the two come together does a person reach God. The right understanding is the understanding that the Self pervades everywhere, that the Self dwells in every hair and pore of the body and in every corner of the universe. Kashmir Shaivism says, "What place is there in which there is no Shiva? What time is there when there is no Shiva?" This is the understanding you must have. Firm and perfect faith should arise in your heart. You should have complete faith in the presence of God and the presence of the Shakti within. Even if a person does not believe that he is a human being, still he is a human being. In the same way, even if a person does not believe that God is within him, still God is there.

Through the power of understanding and the power of contemplation, you should make the feeling of the Self arise within you. No matter what your state, you should not forget that you are the Self. You should always be in the state of nonduality. You should perform your own actions, the actions that you are destined to perform, but you should never consider yourself limited by these actions. You should always maintain the viewpoint of nonduality, which is the viewpoint of the Self.

It is said that the worst sin is to identify with the body, to say, "I am an ordinary person." To have this sort of awareness is the worst hell. But to have the awareness "I am the Self, I am pure, I am sublime" is not only the highest virtue; it is also the best *sadhana*, the *sadhana* that will take you to God. Guru Nanak said very truly, "O man, why do you seek That from forest to forest? He lives within you." God is not without you, nor are you without God. Live your life with this truth. Lead your life in this very truth. This is *sadhana*. This is the experience. This is the state of liberation in life.

Keep Moving On

Once there was a poor woodcutter. All day he would cut down trees and take the wood to the market to sell. He did not care about day or night or heat or cold; he just did his work every day. He worked so hard that he became exhausted. He was so emaciated that his bones and ribs showed. One day as he was wandering unhappily in the forest, he came across a great being. When the great being saw his predicament, he became concerned and said, "O son, don't be so worried. Just go farther." Then he left.

If a person is wise, then even one word is enough for him. But if a person lacks understanding, then even if he is taught the entire scriptures it is still not enough. When the great being said, "Just go farther," the woodcutter said to himself, "All right, I will," and he began to walk. He went farther and farther until he came to a forest filled with sandalwood trees. This sandalwood was worth much more money than the wood that the woodcutter had been taking to market. Now he began to sell sandalwood, and he made a lot of money, but he thought, "Babaji said to go farther." So he walked farther and soon came across a copper mine. With the money he had made selling sandalwood, he hired some people and began to mine the copper and sell it. Now he was earning much more money, but he thought, "Baba said to go farther. I should go farther." And on he went. First he came across a mine of silver and, later, a mine of gold. It was not long before he had become a millionaire, but again he thought, "Babaji told me to go farther. He did not tell me to stop." So on he went until he came across a mine of precious jewels. Now he was a billionaire. People wondered how he had made so much money, but he only kept thinking, "He told me to go farther." He did not stop. One day he met the same *sadhu*. "O my son," said the *sadhu*, "just as you went farther and farther, now go deeper and deeper within."

In the same way, you should keep going farther within until you reach the mine of jewels which is the inner Self. In the beginning, you may have a few *kriyas* or see a few sparkling lights, but this is just the forest of sandalwood trees. You may have some visions or experience a few moments of stillness, but this is just the copper mine. If you want to attain the effulgence of the inner Self, if you want to reach the goal of *sadhana*, you have to keep moving on.

Spiritual Aptitude

Q: A math student may pursue math with great effort, but if he has no innate aptitude he will not attain anything. Isn't this true of students of spirituality? If so, how do I know if I have what it takes?

SM: A student of spirituality should have a burning desire to attain God. No artist, no matter what his field, can attain anything without losing himself in his art. In the same way, you can attain God only if you lose yourself in His love. The moment you have a burning desire, He appears before you. God is right within you — why can't you see Him? It is because you don't have a burning desire.

However, once your Shakti has been awakened, if you keep meditating and chanting and reading the scriptures, through God's grace you will develop an interest in attaining God. Your interest will create an aptitude within and will eventually give rise to a burning desire for God. That burning desire will show you the path of *sadhana*.

The Journey to the Self

Q: I have always heard that the journey to the Self is very painful.

SM: Truly speaking, the journey is not so painful. It is only you who make it painful. Through the help of the Self, the Guru, and knowledge, this journey becomes very joyful; it becomes your friend. In Maharashtra there was a great saint called Eknath Maharaj, whose Guru was a Siddha. Eknath was a very great poet, and he also wrote a commentary on the *Bhagavatam* called the *Eknathi Bhagavatam*. In it Eknath wrote, "I will lead my worldly life with great happiness. I will fill all three worlds with bliss." If you take the help of wisdom, the Self, and the Truth, you can lead your worldly life very easily and with great joy; your spiritual life will also be very easy and joyful. It is completely wrong to say that meditation is difficult. Meditation is the elder brother of sleep; it lies just beyond sleep. The deep sleep state lies beyond the waking and dream states, and the *turiya* state, or the state of meditation, lies beyond the deep sleep state. Meditation is so natural. Just as you prepare yourself to sleep very peacefully, in the same way you should prepare yourself to meditate. Then you will find it very easy and very joyful and very peaceful.

There is nothing greater than meditation; there is no path easier than meditation. Meditation is greater than lectures on spirituality. Those polished words are like the delicious food you read about in a cookbook. If you just keep reading the cookbook and don't cook anything, you will starve to death. That is what people do in spirituality. They go on and on reading books; they don't make the food. Just by reading and reading and listening and listening, you won't attain anything. You should meditate. Meditating is like cooking delicious food; very delicious food is created within you. These days people mainly give talks and seldom act. In Vedanta there is a saying that a person who just keeps talking is like a ladle that doesn't know the taste of *khir*, sweet Indian pudding. *Khir* is served with a long wooden spoon. The spoon makes noise when it serves people. It says, "Take this *khir*, take this *khir*, take this *khir*." It itself doesn't know the taste of the *khir*, but it tells everyone else to take the *khir*. That's what happens when people talk too much about spirituality. They don't get the taste of what they are talking about. So speak little and listen a little and then you can do a lot. If you spend all your time talking and listening, what do you get? Nothing in your hand.

Meditation is absolutely necessary, but you have to meditate in a very disciplined way, just as you go to sleep in a very disciplined manner. You may be an artist, a musician, a professor, a principal, a scholar, a secretary, or a minister, but whatever you are, you go to sleep. When you go to sleep, you feel rested; you experience peace. And in the morning if someone asks you how you slept, you say, "I had a very sound sleep and I feel very satisfied now; all my exhaustion is gone." Just as all your tiredness is removed in your sleep, in the same way you have to meditate to feel the supreme rest. You should meditate and you should awaken your inner Shakti completely. If once the inner Shakti is awakened, it will live with you all the time. Even if you give it up, still it will be with you.

How to Meditate on the Self

Q: Could you explain how to meditate on the Self?

SM: It is not so easy to meditate on the Self, but it is also not so difficult. If you free your mind from thoughts, if you become thoughtless, then you can meditate on your own Self, and also you will come to know how to meditate on the Self. So free your mind from thoughts; then that will be meditation on the Self. The fact is that one can meditate on the Self through the grace of the Self. For this you need a little bit of knowledge. In India there is a great philosophy text called *Jnaneshwari*, and it has been translated into English. You find such books here too, and I have seen many people reading them. In it, Jnaneshwar says, "The light of the Self, the inspiration of the Self always vibrates within you; it is ever new. If you really want to taste the Self, if you really want to attain or see the light of the Self, then you have to steal that light from your own senses." If you let the senses know what you are doing, then you won't be able to taste the Self, you won't be able to taste the sweetness of the Self, you won't be able to see the light of the Self. *Patanjali Yoga Sutras*, the great scripture of yoga, says that to still the mind is yoga; to still the mind is meditation on the Self, and that also teaches you how to meditate on the Self. The fact is that if someone has the right understanding, just by meditating on the Self he comes to know how to meditate on the Self. The *Bhagavad Gita* says, "The Self shines through all your senses." When that is the case, where are you looking for the Self, where are you searching for the Self, and where are you meditating on the Self? The Self just reveals itself through all your senses. But even though the Self shines through all your senses, still it is beyond the senses. None of the senses can reach the Self. The Self is attributeless. It doesn't cast any shadow, it doesn't have any form, and it doesn't have any senses. But even though it is beyond all the senses, still it is the enjoyer, it is the experiencer of all the different objects of the senses. Through these eyes, it is the Self which looks at objects. It is the Self which hears, which listens to all words, and it is the Self which tastes all different kinds of flavors. Man is deluded, and through his delusion he tries to look for God, he tries to see the Self. But truly speaking, God is revealed in His own form; He is not unrevealed.

You never know what delusion is like. Once when Sheikh Nasrudin was walking in the dark, he fell into a pit. The moment he fell, he became scared. It's the nature of the mind that once you become afraid of something, fear just goes on increasing. So Nasrudin became more and more scared. He became so quiet, he was so scared, that he felt he was almost dead. Then be began to think, "No one is here; who will take the message about my accident to my wife?" When he realized there was no one to take the message, he suddenly got up and began to run toward his house. When he got home, he told his wife, "See, I fell into that pit over there, and now I'm almost dead!" Then he ran back to the pit and threw himself into it. He began to shout for help. Now other people came and asked him, "Why are you shouting?" The wife was crying at her house; she was shouting and screaming, and all the neighbors came to ask her, "What's wrong with you? Why are you shouting?" She said, "My husband, Sheikh Nasrudin, is dead!" They asked her, "Where is he?" She said, "Lying in a pit." "Who told you?" they asked. "Nasrudin came and told me, and then he left."

This is the nature of delusion. You also have the delusion of looking for the Self, but truly speaking the Self is already revealed. It is the Self which has taken the form of men and women. The philosophy of Shaivism says, "It is God who takes, and it is God who gives. It is God who eats, and it is God who drinks." Everything is God; God does everything, and God experiences everything. In this universe He plays His drama, and this universe is nothing but Him.

Through meditation you can know your own inner Self. That one who understands the most secret things inside you is the Self. For example, when you are in sleep there is someone who watches everything, who witnesses everything, who understands everything even though you are asleep. And then when you wake up, that being tells you what you have seen in your dream. That being is the Self, so meditate on that inner Self.

Just as You Are Aware of Your Body

Q: My day starts with the telephone ringing, and it keeps on ringing until late into the night. In the course of the day, I find that I forget my Self, that my focus becomes external. Can you suggest some way that I can remember my Self?

SM: No matter how many times the telephone rings, you don't forget your body because the moment you hear the telephone, your hand, which is part of your body, reaches for it. Just as you are aware of your body, you should be aware that the Self is present and that it is allowing you to do all your work. If you cannot do that, then when you have finished your work and are resting, you can remember your Self for a few minutes. That is more than enough.

A man knows that he is a man; he doesn't have to keep repeating the mantra "I am a man, I am a man." A woman knows that she is a woman; she doesn't have to keep repeating the mantra "I am a woman, I am a woman." Similarly, once you become aware that you are the Self, you don't have to keep repeating "I am the Self, I am the Self."

Dealing with the Mind

Q: Why is it that when I try to meditate on the mantra, rivers of thoughts come into my mind simultaneously, making it nearly impossible to concentrate. And after a short period, my knees, lower back, and neck begin to ache mercilessly. What can I do?

SM: Your knees begin to ache because you don't have the habit of sitting on the floor for a long time in one position. You can sit on a chair, or you can just stretch out your legs and keep meditating or doing your *japa*. For a while you should be very stubborn in repeating the mantra. If you persist in repeating the mantra, then the mischief of the mind will stop. Then everything will be fine. The mind has the habit of wandering here and there, of fluctuating all the time, and because it has had this habit for a long time, it is very difficult for the mind to become still. But you should never give any freedom to your mind. You shouldn't let the mind go wherever it feels like. You should catch hold of the mind, pull it back, and make it repeat

God's name. You should make it meditate, and you should make it have only pure and good thoughts. The mind is the root of pain and pleasure for human beings. There is no other reason for you to experience pain and pleasure; it is the mind which makes you experience these things. Sometimes it shows you joy in sorrow and makes you suffer in that way, and sometimes it shows you sorrow in joy and makes you suffer in that way. That is why you shouldn't chase the mind. Instead, you should make the mind pursue the Self. You are not made up of that mind; the mind is made up of you, and it is within you. There are so many people who feel weak and feeble because they have been defeated by their own minds, the minds they have created in themselves. Even if a person conquers an entire country, he is not a conqueror if he has not conquered his mind. That is why you should be very careful about your mind. You should always watch your mind; you should know if the mind is having good thoughts or not. Among all these senses and instruments, the mind is the greatest. The more still it becomes, the more stabilized it is, the more pure it becomes, and the greater and more ideal you become. But when the mind becomes agitated by petty thoughts and feelings, then you have to go to a psychologist or a psychic. That is why you should make your mind pure. You should free your mind from hatred and other defects; you should clean your mind, and you should make it clearer.

Learning to Sit

Q: During meditation, I often experience physical pain in my legs. In other yogas I have done I've been told not to move, to endure the pain. While meditating, is it more important that I move and be more comfortable or that I endure the pain?

SM: When your legs begin to ache in meditation, you can change your position. Put your upper leg below and your lower leg above, but do not move your trunk. Mastery of the sitting posture is necessary for meditation. If you want to master a posture, you must not move. Whatever pain you feel will continue to occur for only a few days. You should learn to endure pain little by little. If you begin to experience pain in the sitting posture after half an hour, continue to bear it for five more minutes and then relax your legs. After a week of that you will find that you can sit for thirty-five minutes without feeling any pain. Keep on extending the duration in this way, and you will be able to sit longer in a posture.

Once one acquires the ability to sit in the lotus posture without moving at all for one hour and forty-five minutes, then one acquires mastery of *prana*. The mind becomes steady. When the mind becomes steady, one glides into *sahajasamadhi*, or spontaneous *samadhi*. So mastery of the sitting position is essential. Increase your duration little by little, for example, five minutes every week. After a month you will be able to sit twenty minutes longer, and after two months forty minutes longer. There is no discipline a human being cannot learn.

The Real Attainment

Q: Why does one fall back into ignorance even after seeing one's true nature?

SM: After seeing one's true nature, one should become established in it; otherwise, one falls. Because your true nature exists within you, you can experience it easily and spontaneously. However, becoming established in your true nature after seeing it requires practice. For example, you experience happiness many times during the day, even if only for a few seconds, but those experiences of happiness slip away because you never practice any *sadhana* to make them last.

In *Patanjali Yoga Sutras* it is said that after you experience the happiness of your own true nature, you should become anchored in it. Do not forget it. Practice it.

Learn how to make the mind still in the inner Self. If you have seen That, if you make the mind still in That, then happiness will arise within you. If the mind once again starts wandering outside, it will take on the form of whatever exists outside, and happiness will vanish. If you do not have firm determination and firm practice, then you will fall.

Due to attachment, aversion, anger, and greed, a person falls back into ignorance again and again. You should be steadfast. In the *Bhagavad Gita* it is said that you should become completely established in That. As long as you don't attain the state of witness-consciousness, or steady wisdom, you will rise and fall many times. Therefore, the great beings do not give much importance to just seeing their true nature. The real attainment is the state of witness-consciousness, in which a person becomes established in his true nature, in which the seer becomes still in the seen. When a person attains this state, when he becomes steady in the awareness "I am the Truth," he becomes complete.

How Much Meditation?

Q: In your autobiography, *Play of Consciousness*, you say that you meditated for six to nine hours each day. How can a person who lives in the world and who works each day do the same? Can a householder realize what you have realized?

SM: An hour or an hour and a half of meditation each day is enough. You do not have to meditate too much. If you are a householder and cannot find time to meditate during the day, you can meditate before you fall asleep. Fall asleep while pursuing *So'ham*, and *So'ham* will continue to take place even as you sleep, until you wake up in the morning. It is not that you need to meditate for six to nine hours every day. The experience of the Self is the same for everybody. This experience exists inside everybody. It doesn't come from outside. Therefore, go deep, deep inside. The great ancient sages were all householders. In this world there are many householders who pursue a spiritual life. Meditation does not interfere with daily life. If you think that it is an obstacle in your daily life, then you are not thinking correctly. Whoever you are, you can meditate; then, certainly, you will attain That. Even though it is already attained, even though you already have it, it is very important to become established in it.

Blocks Along the Path

Q: There seem to be blocks along the spiritual path. Why is this so?

SM: Is the path of the mundane world free of blocks? Look at your own life. How many psychologists have you had? How many doctors?

How many enemies? When there are so many difficulties on the mundane path, why should the spiritual path be easy? Nonetheless, the spiritual path is much easier than the mundane path. On this path you do not have to quarrel or fight. All you have to do is turn inside and meditate peacefully on the Self.

When you are doing *sadhana* it is very natural for obstacles to arise, but you should not attach any importance to them. The inner Shakti will take care of them. You should only pursue your *sadhana*.

Conquering the Inner Enemies

Q: What is the purpose of endurance and of doing *tapasya* (austerities)?

SM: The word *tapas* literally means "heating." A person performs austerities in order to heat the senses, to control them, to make them his slaves rather than being enslaved by them. There are inner enemies and outer enemies. The inner enemies are anger, lust, desire, and so on. The outer enemies are the senses, which act on those feelings. To conquer both the inner and outer enemies is the purpose of *tapasya*. In ancient times people performed very severe austerities, but this is not necessary. For us, the greatest austerity is to discipline the mind by engaging it in the repetition of God's names. Speaking the truth is also a great austerity. So is not being a nuisance to anyone and not being hostile to anyone. However, the best *tapasya* you can practice is to lead your life with the awareness of God's existence within your heart.

Endurance is the power to tolerate anything. No matter what pain you come across, digest it with joy. Accept it not under compulsion, but with great pleasure. Tolerate heat and cold, pain and pleasure. When it is cold, do not feel too cold; when it is hot, do not feel too hot. When there is pain, do not suffer too much; when there is pleasure, do not enjoy it too much. If you are able to remain uninvolved with these pairs of opposites, then you have the power of endurance. Truly speaking, you can live happily only when you have the power of endurance. Whether you want to or not, you have to endure discomfort and pain in this world. You do bear all these things. However, you bear them not with happiness, but with unhappiness. If you learn how to endure these things, then you will be able to remain calm and happy even in the worst difficulties.

Endurance and willingness to undergo *tapasya* are the signs of a seeker. In the *Bhagavad Gita* the Lord says, "Only he is a yogi who remains steady in both pain and pleasure." Therefore, practice developing these qualities.

The Center of Fear

Q: Why, in the course of *sadhana*, does one go through periods of feeling frightened?

SM: When you go on an external journey, you come across broken roads and you go through thick forests. In the same way, when you are on the inner journey, you come across different sorts of places. Just as there is a center of love within you, there is also a center of fear. There is a veil between the individual soul and the supreme Self, and this veil represents fear. As your awareness moves closer and closer to the supreme Self you experience this fear. You become terrified of letting yourself go. It is that fear which stops you from becoming one with Him. Sometimes a meditator gives up meditating forever because he becomes so terrified when he comes across the center of fear. You should watch out for this center of fear. If you can face it, you will go beyond it. Then you will become completely fearless. If you lose yourself with great courage, you will attain That. If you hold yourself back because of that fear, you will lose everything.

There was a great saint called Shams-i-Tabriz. Shams means "the sun," and he was called Shams because he was always shining like the sun. He said, "If you want to attain Him, then you should lose your individuality in Him." The ego is your worst enemy, so you should obliterate this ego. If you want to attain something great, then eradicate your individuality. You are not going to attain Him if you maintain your individuality. Only if you lose yourself will you attain Him. Do not get stuck in a particular condition or in your wrong understanding. Give up your wrong understanding. Then you will merge into Him.

Shams-i-Tabriz gave a beautiful analogy, saying, "A grain of wheat merges into the earth. It loses itself there completely. Then once again it sprouts; it becomes a beautiful plant and then it has so many grains of wheat."

As long as your ego exists, as long as your individuality exists, you cannot attain God. Once your individuality is obliterated, you are God.

The Pace of Sadhana

Q: Should the pace of my sadhana be forced, or should I let it unfold at its own natural pace?

SM: Let your sadhana increase naturally. Let it happen spontaneously. Sadhana should increase in a disciplined manner. You have to have great strength and energy for sadhana to go forward with great force.

Once Lord Buddha was sitting on the bank of a river doing very hard tapasya, when some musicians passed by. They were singing, "O musician, don't keep the strings of the violin too loose, because no tune will come forth. Don't keep the strings too tight; either they will break, or they won't create any melody. Therefore be moderate."

When Buddha heard this song, he realized that he should not observe austere and strenuous tapasya but that he should just meditate naturally and contemplate the Self.

It is not very difficult to enhance your sadhana. It all depends on your feelings. If you want to make your sadhana very strong, you should consider yourself to be the image of Parashiva or a part of Consciousness. That's all you have to do. Then your sadhana will become complete.

The Right Environment

Q: Is it necessary to live in a particular environment to realize the Self?

SM: The right environment is very important for spiritual growth. But by this I do not mean a physical environment; I mean the mental environment of the inward-turned mind. "Environment" to me does not signify a cave or a solitary spot; it means always staying centered inside. In our present state we are conscious of ourselves as the body, but for Self-realization it is necessary that we be conscious of being the Self, not the body. No matter what I say, the essence of all my teachings is that you should stay focused on the inner Self. You don't have to change your home or your society or even your manners. All that you need to change is your understanding of yourself. Always remain aware of yourself as the Self. That is the essence of all spiritual teachings.

Let Them Tease You

Q: I have heard you say how important it is for someone who is practicing spiritual *sadhana* to be with others who are experiencing spiritual growth. I am longing for Self-realization but find my path frequently blocked because I am married to someone who enjoys drinking and a fast social pace. He and our friends tease me about my dedication to yoga and the fact that I no longer wish to live the way they do. He is sometimes cruel, blaming me for being strange because of my beliefs. How do you advise married couples who are growing in separate directions? What can one do without hurting one's spouse?

SM: You should not hurt your husband, but you can tell him very fondly that just as he is interested in drinking and a fast social life, you are interested in yoga. Tell him that if he is willing to give up his interests, you will give up yours. Tell him that just as he cannot give up his addictions because he is very fond of them, you are very fond of your addiction to yoga and cannot give it up. If others can't give up their addictions, why should we give up our addiction?

One day Tulsidas was having a bath in the Ganga. A scorpion came floating along with the current. Tulsidas was filled with pity and picked up the scorpion. The scorpion bit him hard, fell off his hand, and began to float once again in the water. Again Tulsidas picked up the scorpion, and again it bit him. This happened ten times.

A man who had been watching all this from the river bank called to Tulsidas, "Hey, what kind of person are you? This low, wicked, degraded scorpion has bitten you ten times and yet you want to save its life. Why don't you let him meet his fate?"

Tulsidas replied, "Brother, even when its life is at stake the scorpion is not acting against its nature. When my life is not at stake, why should I act against my nature?" So if they cannot give up their ways, why should we give up ours?

The scriptures say that to people who have turned away from God, those who have a strong spiritual interest look like evil spirits or ghosts. Likewise, to people who are interested in yoga, those who are not interested appear to be like ghosts. The scriptures say that what is day for the owl is night for the crow and vice versa. Let your husband and friends tease you. Why should you let that disturb you?

Once someone started swearing at Lord Buddha. Buddha listened calmly. When the man tired of swearing and fell silent, Buddha asked him, "If you invited guests to your house and cooked food for them, and if they did not eat it, what would you do?"

The man replied, "I come from a very respectable family, and we have many guests. If they do not eat the food we have cooked, I myself eat it."

"I have not eaten all the swearing that you hurled at me," replied Buddha. "Now you will have to eat it."

So let them tease you, but do not let their words enter your heart. Just continue your practice of yoga.

The Worst Company

Q: You teach that it is not good to keep bad company. What do you recommend for someone who works in a prison?

SM: I have good advice for you. Truly speaking, there is not such bad company in prison. Instead of worrying about that bad company, change your inner bad company because outside you can always make it better.

You come into contact with prisoners sometimes, but what about the bad company that lives within you? You are always in contact with that company, so improve that company from within.

The Bhagavad Gita says that the inner enemies, desire and anger, are the worst company. You should conquer these enemies. A great being said, "Desire, anger, pride, and greed are the worst enemies. O man, run away from them."

These are the bad company you should leave. It is all right to work in prison, but do not become a prisoner.

Every Place Can Be a Holy Place: A Message to Prisoners

You are behind walls. For a while, you are being punished for your actions. However, you should understand that the place where you are living right now is a purificatory place. You came here with all your sins and faults, but when you leave you will be free of all faults. You will be pure. In India there are holy rivers, and it is said that if you take a bath in them you become free of sins. In the same way, your jail is also a holy place.

You must have heard of Mahatma Gandhi. He learned the teaching of peace and nonviolence in prison and came out of prison as a great being who freed India without using any weapons. There was another great leader called Lokmanya Tilak who was also imprisoned. The great yogi Aurobindo became enlightened when he was in jail. The composer of the *Bhagavad Gita*, Lord Krishna, was an incarnation of God, and he was born in a prison.

In order to practice spiritual pursuits, people look for a place that appears like a prison, a place where nobody comes and where nobody will bother them. However, they don't call themselves prisoners. They call themselves lovers of solitude. If you think very carefully, you will realize that by leading you to prison, God has given you an opportunity to think of your own Self and to remember God. In prison you lead a disciplined life. You get your food on time. You go to bed on time. You get your clothes on time. Even while living in a jail one can pursue spiritual practice, one can meditate, one can think of one's inner Self. Therefore, do not belittle a jail.

Everything depends upon your attitude. If you change your attitude toward a place, then no matter where you are, that place becomes heaven for you. If you have full faith in God, if you have full faith in the truth that whatever happens to you happens according to the will of God, then every place, every moment, and every event of your life will begin to feel sublime.

Once there was a great prime minister in India who had this

kind of understanding. If a parent said to him, "My son has died," he would say, "Good. Whatever God does is for the best." If a woman said to him, "My husband died," he would say, "Good. Whatever God does is for the best." People reacted violently against him. They thought he was crazy and were constantly hatching plots to remove him from power.

One day the king was being shaved by his barber and happened to doze off. While cutting his nails, the barber accidentally cut off the tip of his finger. The prime minister's enemies thought that this was a wonderful opportunity to teach him a lesson. They rushed to him and said, "Prime minister, the barber has cut off the king's finger." The prime minister said, "Good. Whatever God does is for the best." The prime minister's enemies went to the king and told him what the prime minister said. The king called the prime minister into his presence and said, "You fool. You have been eating my food and living on my money, and now you have the nerve to say that it's a good thing my finger was cut off?" He ordered his men to put the prime minister in jail and to give him only dry bread to eat. "Now you'll see whether what God does is for the best," he said.

The prime minister sat locked up in his cell and calmly remembered God's name. He wasn't upset, and when people would go to visit him and ask him, "How are you? he would say, "Very good. God has put me here and it is good for me."

A few days later, the king went off to the forest to hunt. On his way he met a gang of bandits whose leader was a worshipper of the goddess Kali. The bandit leader needed to sacrifice an important person to the goddess, so he kidnapped the king and dragged him to the temple as a sacrificial offering. The bandits examined the king thoroughly to see if his body was whole, because only one whose body is perfect can be sacrificed to the goddess. As they were examining him, they noticed that the tip of his finger was cut and said, "His body is impure. He is not worthy of the goddess." So the king was released. Immediately he realized that if his finger had not been cut he would have lost his head. He remembered that the prime minister had said, "Whatever God does is for the best," and recognized that he had been right.

The king returned to his capital and had the prime minister released from his cell. When the prime minister came before him, he told him what had happened and then asked, "It was good for me that my finger was cut, but how was it good for you to have been locked inside this cell, living on dry crumbs?"

The prime minister replied, "Your majesty, if you had not locked me in this cell, I would have gone hunting with you, and the bandits would have also grabbed me. They released you because your finger was cut, but they would have sacrificed me because my body is whole. Whatever God does is for the best."

If that could be your attitude in prison, then prison would be like heaven, not like hell. Our experience of the world depends on our understanding. Because of your narrow understanding you must be experiencing a lot of pain, but you should realize that it is not only you who are experiencing this pain. You may think that only you are a prisoner, but other people are also prisoners. You are in a small prison, but other people are in the big prison outside. When will they be released?

All these people are bound by their own narrow understanding and by the noose of their karma, the consequences of what they have done. A wealthy person is bound by the noose of his wealth. A poor person is bound by the noose of his poverty. An officeholder is bound by the pride of his office. A great leader is bound by the noose of his own leadership, and a person in authority is bound by the noose of his own authority. Everyone who lives in this world is a prisoner. What about the policemen and guards who are here with you? Of course, they don't think that they are prisoners, but what do they experience? What about the jailer who has power over you? Is he happy? You are all in the same place. So change your understanding. Think that you are a yogi and that you are pursuing your sadhana in this particular place and at this particular moment. Immediately you will experience great joy.

You may have made many mistakes. Because you are within these walls, you remember them. People who are outside also make mistakes, but since they don't consider themselves prisoners they forget them. The difference lies in your understanding. Your entire mental condition is based on the understanding that you are a prisoner, and because of that understanding, painful thoughts arise and you keep burning within. If you change your understanding, you will be free in a minute. If you develop love for God, then even while living in a prison you will be a priest.

Become absorbed in the thought of Consciousness, the thought of God, just as now you are absorbed in the thought of being a prisoner. Sit quietly with great peace. Try to know yourself, and waves of joy will arise inside you. Experience Consciousness above you, below you, behind you. Inside, there is great divinity. Just as a person absorbed in deep sleep doesn't experience pleasure or pain, only great peace, so one who is absorbed in meditation does not experience the pleasures or pain of the outer world. He experiences only the bliss of heaven.

It is with great respect and great love that I welcome you all with all my heart. I don't say this out of sympathy with you because you are in jail. I say this with the understanding that the God who is in me is also in you. If you direct your attention within, you will discover Him and be transformed.

4

Discipline

Discipline Is the Root of Yoga

In order to pursue *sadhana* successfully, you have to have a lot of strength and a lot of energy. Only then will your *sadhana* go forward with great force. People think that a person who meditates is inactive because he is always sitting very still, but the truth is that during meditation you use up a lot of energy. For this reason a disciplined life is absolutely necessary. Through discipline and regularity you can conserve the strength in your body and make it grow, so that you can use it for the pursuit of God.

God has placed the same power in all bodies. There is no partiality in God's distribution; He has given us as much power as He has kept for Himself. However, we waste the energy God has given us through the senses and the mind. As we do this, we become weaker and weaker. A car may be guaranteed for three years, but if the owner drives the car day and night, will it really last for three years? But if the owner drives it for a limited amount of time every day, and if he takes very good care of it, then it may last not only for three years but for twelve. In the same way, if you keep your body very disciplined, if you never let it become lazy, then it will become very strong and you will be able to accomplish a lot. Most people drive their body and senses day and night. They keep looking at things that it is not necessary for them to see. They keep listening to things that it is not necessary for them to hear. Above all, they think so many unnecessary and useless thoughts. In this way, their energy is scattered, so that they become weaker and weaker.

A yogi does not scatter his energy like this. Instead, he trains his eyes to see only good things. He trains his ears to hear only good things. He trains his tongue to eat moderately and to speak only as much as is necessary. He keeps his body strong through hard physical work. Above all, he keeps his mind one-pointed. Every day he meditates and repeats the mantra and tries to make the mind still. In this way, his energy is not wasted, but remains within him and grows.

Discipline is the root of yoga. The *Bhagavad Gita* says, "Success in yoga is barred to one who eats too much or not at all, who sleeps too much or not at all." Only a person who remains moderate and disciplined, who does not overeat, who does not sell himself to sleep, who makes his senses his slaves instead of becoming enslaved by them can succeed in yoga.

Not only a person who practices yoga needs discipline in his life. Discipline is important for anyone who wants to lead a happy life. Unless a person controls the senses, what kind of life can he lead? When a person chases after the senses, he forgets his Self. He forgets what exists and remembers what does not exist. In his heart he always feels that he lacks something; he never feels fulfilled. If a person is not self-controlled, he becomes a slave; his life becomes dependent on outer things. Then he finds his happiness in pills and doctors, and weeps and wails over his fate.

Look at your own life. You have always done everything according to your own whims. You have eaten when you wanted to, you have slept when you wanted to, you have done exactly what you wanted to do. What have you attained by this? Can you answer this? If you are frank, the only things you can say that you have attained are agitation and distress. This is the only answer a sensible person can give. You are disturbed by even a little bit of pain and discomfort. Your mind becomes upset whenever anything goes wrong. Is this not the case? This is the result of lack of discipline.

When a person has no self-control, he has no ability to endure hardship. He weeps when he has to face sickness or other worldly difficulties. All people have to experience pain in their lives. But while an ordinary person faces difficulties weeping and complaining, a person who has developed self-control can endure anything joyfully. He has the strength to bear the worst difficulties with equanimity. For this reason, discipline is a great attainment and a great friend.

A life of discipline is nectar; it is filled with joy. The scriptures say that in the beginning, a disciplined life may seem very strenuous and painful but that as you pursue it, it soon becomes joyful. On the other hand, the pleasures that give you momentary joy bring sorrow and trouble in the future. The joys of the senses are short-lived, but the joy you attain through discipline lasts a lifetime. Take my case, for example. During my *sadhana*, I put forth a lot of effort and followed very strict discipline. Now I am in the ocean of joy. The pain of my *sadhana* has become nectar for me now. But so many wealthy people come to see me, leaning on two canes. They have money, they have cars, they have beautiful houses, they have everything. Still, they stand in front of me and put their heads in both their hands and cry. The joy they once found in sense pleasures has become the disease of their old age. A person should think about this a lot, and after contemplating this, he should decide what kind of life he wants to lead.

Therefore, be disciplined in your life. Go to sleep punctually at night, get up at the same time every day, eat at a regular hour, go to your office at the right time. Speak only as much as is absolutely necessary. Eat only what you need to sustain life; do not overload your stomach. Do everything in moderation. Do not become the victim of addictions. Even if your pleasures are harmless, have the detachment not to need them all the time. This is the kind of life a yogi should lead.

It is really not difficult to develop regular habits, because there is no science or wisdom that a human being cannot learn. At first, it may take effort to follow a particular discipline, but later your mind, body, and senses will get into the habit of it and it will become easy. For example, many Westerners complain to me that they have difficulty sitting with their legs crossed. But after they have practiced this posture for a few months, increasing the duration little by little, they can do it with no trouble. In the same way, people often have a hard time getting up early in the morning for meditation, because all their lives they have been sleeping late. But after they have done it for a while, their bodies become so accustomed to waking up early that it happens automatically. A human being is a creature of habit. Whatever habit he establishes soon becomes second nature to him. Once you have established a particular discipline for yourself, it will soon become natural to you.

But in order for your external and internal discipline to become firm, you must have the tendency of renunciation. Renunciation does not mean having to give up your household life, your family, or your children. It means being self-restrained and in control of your senses. You can never control the body and senses without controlling the desires that always play in your mind. The *Bhagavad Gita* says that desire and anger are the constant enemies of wisdom. Only when they are controlled can the mind become still.

Once King Akbar took it into his head to train some cats. In those days there was no electricity and, for light, people would burn lamps in small clay pots. Akbar trained four cats to carry these lamps on their heads and stand still while he was eating his meals. He thought that he had done a great thing, and he was very proud of himself for having trained the cats so well.

One day he invited his prime minister Birbal to take a look at his achievement. Birbal was very intelligent. When he went to the king's dining room and saw the cats with the lamps on their heads, he said, "Your Majesty, before I can be certain whether these cats have really been trained, I will have to put them to a test. With your permission I will come back tomorrow."

The next day, Birbal brought a rat in his pocket. When the king sat down for his meal, Birbal took the rat out and put it on the floor. The moment the cats spotted the rat, they forgot all of their training. They jumped up, spilled the oil lamps on the floor, and began to chase the rat.

This is what happens to our minds when we do not control our desires. Even though we may try to meditate or maintain a particular discipline, our past impressions and the force of our desires remain so strong that if we leave them alone they will lead us around by the nose. Unless we control them, the mind will never become still.

Nowadays, most people do not like the idea of controlling their desires. Modern psychologists have told them that if they repress their desires they will feel frustrated and might even become ill. I have met many psychologists who say that the only way you can find peace is to act out all of your desires. They say that if you fulfill your desires they will leave you in peace. The sages, however, knew that if you give way to your desires you will never find peace, but only more agitation. You can never fulfill your desires by indulging in them, any more than you can put out a fire by pouring oil on it. If you try to satisfy one desire, another one will spring up, and if you try to satisfy that desire, a third one will come in its place. If you keep trying to satisfy your desires, they will blaze up higher and higher until finally they swallow you completely. The only way to become peaceful is to become free of desires, and the only way to become free of desires is to recognize and control them.

For this reason, it is said that a person who wants to succeed in yoga should cultivate detachment and the tendency of renunciation. When desires come up in the mind, one must be able to let them go. This is what discipline means. The senses always want to go outward, toward the objects of desire. The mind follows the senses, and therefore it is constantly wandering here and there, losing itself in the outer world. Instead of letting the mind and senses go wherever they choose, a disciplined person fights with them. He pulls the mind back from the objects of desire. He brings it back from its wanderings and makes it centered on the mantra. He turns it inward, toward the Self, which is beyond all senses and all objects. If he does this again and again, if he makes the mind taste the nectar that is in the Self, it becomes easier and easier for him to make the mind quiet.

True discipline is discipline of the mind. True self-control is control over the wanderings of the mind. Even though at first you will have to work hard to make the mind disciplined, even though you will have to oppose its tendencies with great strength, the time will come when it will become accustomed to turning inward, and then you will begin to swim in the ocean of tranquility that surrounds the Self.

The Greatest Discipline

Q: I am troubled because every time I try to make myself adhere to greater discipline or bring my desires under control, I do the opposite of what I expect of myself. How can I bring my actions more in tune with my ideals?

SM: You have to change your thoughts and actions. Man should not be at the mercy of his thoughts. He shouldn't be controlled by his thoughts. Weakness of mind makes your life full of suffering; there is no life that is more miserable. The greatest problem in life is the problem of the wandering mind. A person doesn't become unhappy because he lacks wealth or education. I have seen people who lacked food or clothes who were happy, but I have never seen a person whose mind was disturbed who was happy.

With great courage, struggle to change your mind and to make it become established in a better place. Then you will become very happy. To struggle in this way is to observe the greatest discipline, and to do so you have to become a great warrior. The Upanishads say that only a courageous person can become established in the Self. Such a person becomes peaceful and is freed from all worries. You are not under the control of your mind; you only think that you are under its control. Just as when you blow your nose to discard the dirt in your nostrils, in the same way you can eliminate your negative thoughts. Just throw them away. This instant, right now, try to bring your mind under control.

The mind is such that if you remain conscious of the shortness of your life and of the value of time, then your mind will automatically become calm and your desires will remain under control.

I am reminded of a story about Eknath Maharaj. Eknath's ashram was always full of activity, and every day he would serve sweets to the many people who were fed there. One day a millionaire came to meet Eknath, and when he saw the saint sitting calmly and cheerfully, unagitated in the midst of so much activity, he was surprised. He said, "If I held such a big feast I would have to plan it well in advance. I would need many assistants and assistants to assist the assistants, and even then I might not succeed. So many things are going on around here and yet you are so calm. What is your secret?"

Eknath pretended not to hear the question. Instead, he snapped at the man, "You are going to die within seven days! Now get out of here!"

The millionaire immediately forgot about his question. He was horrified by what he had heard. His shock was so great that he couldn't even walk and had to be carried away in a *tonga*. It is not surprising that this man collapsed when he heard that he was going to die in seven days, because he had never remembered God. He had never taken an interest in anything spiritual. He had not earned steadfastness or courage. He had only been absorbed in earning more and more money, which he could not take with him at his death.

The millionaire was taken home and laid on his bed. He called his relatives and told them the news. Whenever he thought of his death, he began to groan. "Alas! Alas!" he would say. "I have earned so much money. I have shared it with my family and neighbors and still I have so much, but I can't save myself from dying. Alas! Alas!" He could not stop crying and screaming.

As the days passed, he languished more and more. He lost his eyesight, and his other senses deteriorated. Actually, his death was still a long way away; he had become so distressed merely because Eknath had told him he was going to die.

The seventh day arrived. It was eleven o'clock, and the man was convinced that he had only one hour to live. He had become quite calm and still. His mind had stopped wandering, and he had become completely focused. He had lost interest in everything outside himself; his mind was absorbed in the thought that he had only one hour left to live and that the moment the clock struck noon he would perish. Just before twelve, Eknath came in to the room, chanting "*Shri Ram, Jai Ram, Jai Jai Ram.*" The millionaire was very happy to see Eknath because he considered it auspicious to see a saint at the time of death.

"How are you sir?" Eknath asked. "You appear to be quite calm. What is the condition of your mind?"

"How can my mind wander? Only a few minutes are left for me to live, so my mind is completely absorbed in thoughts of death. I am only remembering the Lord."

Eknath said "It is the same with me. I remain perfectly calm, remembering the Lord constantly. I do not think of my wife, sons, brothers, or other relations or the achievements and talents that pertain only to my body. I always remain conscious of death. Who knows when it may strike!"

Thought and desires will arise in the mind only if you are not conscious of death and the value of time. If you make yourself keenly aware of the value of time, you will not let your mind remain restless and distracted. It was for this reason that the great saint Nipat Niranjin said, "Always remember two things. One is God; the other is your own death."

Going Beyond Desires

Q: Is there a way to reverse past desires so we don't have to live through them? Or must we come back to live through every one of them?

SM: To fulfill your desires, you should have only one desire, the desire to spend time with a being who is beyond all desires. Your desires can never be fulfilled if you indulge them. If you try to satisfy one desire, another will spring up, and if you try to satisfy that one, a third will come. There is absolutely no end to all the desires that come up; they keep piling up until they become as huge as a mountain. Desires cannot be fulfilled by indulging them. You can get rid of them only by recognizing them.

Tukaram Maharaj has given the secret of going beyond desire in his poetry. He says that the only way to go beyond desires is to focus all of your desires on the Lord. You should seek all sense enjoyments in the Lord. If you want to see something, see the Lord's form. If you want to hear anything, hear the sound of His name. If you want to touch something, touch His divine form. In this way, find fulfillment of all your desires in Him and through Him, and then you will go beyond all desires.

If you do *arati* to desires all the time, you will never be able to get rid of them. However, if you always keep remembering the inner Self, which is beyond all desires, you will certainly go beyond all desires.

Mind Control

Q: How can I control the mind and its thoughts?

SM: If you really want to bring your mind under your control, you should make it one-pointed by giving it some work to do. Once there was a person who had propitiated a demon with a mantra he had received. The demon said, "I will work for you, but you must agree to one condition: I have to have work all the time. If you cannot give me enough work, I will eat you up." The man was terrified. Every day he gave the demon more and more work, but the demon was a very fast worker. Finally, the work ran out; there was no more to give him.

When a person is in trouble, he looks for a good person to give him some advice, but when he is not in trouble, he never looks for a good person. If he did, he would not have any problems. This man ran to the being who had given him the mantra and said, "Please help me! Save me from this demon!"

"What's the matter?" the great being asked.

"I have run out of work for the demon to do and now I am in real trouble," answered the man.

"Don't be afraid," the sage said. "Go back home and put up a pole forty feet tall. Then tell the demon to keep going up and down the pole. That will keep him busy."

The demon began to do the work of going up and down, up and down the pole, and the man was able to relax. So if you really want to control your mind, you should erect a pole out of the mantra. Tell your devil, your mind, to keep doing the mantra *So'ham*. As it climbs up and down that pole, it will become quiet. This is the best means of controlling your mind.

You Are What You Eat

In Ayurveda, the Indian system of medicine, the question is raised, "Who remains free of disease?" Once the great physician Chanak, the founder of the Ayurvedic system, decided to test his students. He took the form of a bird and soared over the students, repeating, "*Kora ruk? Kora ruk? Kora ruk?* Who stays free of disease? Who stays free of disease? Who stays free of disease?"

Among the students were many clever doctors, and one said, "If you were to take some special variety of fish and cook it and spice it well, you would enjoy wonderful health." Another said, "If you were to eat mutton, you would have continuous good health." A third said, "If you were to eat French chocolates, they would give you extra energy." Chanak was disgusted by these answers and flew away.

The next day he alighted on a tree, under which another group of students were sitting. He shouted the same question: "*Kora ruk?*" The student who was his greatest disciple got up and said, "*Rita buk, mita buk, hita buk.* Only he can stay free of disease who eats frugally, who eats food he can digest, and who eats food that suits the season."

This is absolutely true. Whether you are a yogi or a worldly person, diet is of the greatest importance. The sages say that it is food which nourishes and builds us up and that it is also food which kills us. Food is life and food is death; food is health and food is disease. For this reason, the scriptures tell us that we should always be aware of what we are eating and understand it very well. Moderation is tremendously important. The less restraint we exercise in the matter of food, the more we relax our self-control, the more diseases we will have. It is because people do not exercise self-control in eating that the number of hospitals is increasing in the world. The sages say that when we eat we should fill our stomachs half full of food and a quarter full of water and leave a quarter empty for the free circulation of *prana*. If we do that, we will never have to take refuge in a doctor.

We should have great understanding about food, because food is the life of the individual soul. This body is made of food. From the subtle essence of food, semen is created; and from semen, this body is created. So the individual takes birth due to the subtle essence of food—the semen—and then throughout his life he lives on food. In fact, the Upanishads say, "Consider food the form of God. Have respect for food."

Every kind of food has its own characteristics. Therefore, when you eat any particular food, you should first ask yourself why you are eating it. A yogi needs very pure food, food that has life in it, food that has energy in it. Cereals, fruit, vegetables, and milk are all very good for a person who meditates. These foods are not only nourishing, but easily digestible, and this is very important. Food is digested by means of the same Shakti through whose power you meditate. If you eat a heavy meal that takes six hours to digest, what Shakti will you have left over for meditation?

Not only is your body created by food; food also affects the state of your mind. Whatever quality a certain food has permeates your entire system. For this reason, the sages emphasize that the food you eat should be filled with good impressions, from the time that it is growing to the time it is cooking to the time it is eaten. A person has his own vibration, which pervades everything he touches and everything around him. It pervades his clothes, his bed, his books, and his food. The vibrations of the place in which food is prepared, as well as of the person who handles it, go into that food.

Those vibrations are absorbed into the system of the person who eats it.

There is a true story that illustrates how the vibrations in the food a person eats affect his inner state. Once there was a Jain *bikshu* who was a great renunciant. He lived very close to the palace of a king. In India, renunciants are very much respected, and householders are supposed to serve them and give them whatever they need. The king had great devotion for this mendicant, so one day he asked him to stay in his palace for a while. The mendicant stayed for some months with the king and ate the king's food. After a while his mental condition became just like the king's. It took on the quality of *rajas*, passion. One day as he was walking in the palace he passed the queen's room and saw a beautiful necklace. He felt a desire to have it, so he went into the room and put it in his pocket. For a while everyone searched for the missing necklace, but no one could find it, and at last it was forgotten.

In the meantime, the mendicant left and went to stay in a field. There a poor farmer invited him for a meal. Farmers in India eat a lot of chilies, and this farmer made a vegetable dish full of chilies and served it to the mendicant. After eating the chilies, the mendicant got diarrhea. Chilies clean the stomach out very well; that is why they should be eaten sparingly.

The mendicant went to the doctor for some medicine to control his diarrhea, but by mistake the doctor gave him a medicine that made it worse. The worse it got, the more pills the mendicant took, and the more pills he took, the worse his diarrhea became. In this way, the essence of food, of which his body was composed, was washed away. The mendicant was lying on his bed, wondering and contemplating, when suddenly he saw the necklace before his eyes. "Alas, I stole the queen's necklace," he thought. He began to feel very remorseful. He said to himself, "The king served me for three or four months with so much respect and love. What I have done is no good at all."

Even if someone has performed bad actions, if he repents, then he will regain his true nature and begin to perform good actions once again. The mendicant took the necklace to the palace and set it in front of the king. The king was surprised. "O king of mendicants, where did you find this?" he asked.

"I went to a farmer's house and there I began to have diarrhea, and in due course of time I found it."

The king did not understand what he meant. He asked, "What are you saying?"

"O king," said the mendicant, "I stole the necklace."

"But how could a being like you do such a thing?"

"I stayed in your palace for four months. I ate your food, and my mind was affected by it. You perform actions according to the state of your mind. A king is always dissatisfied with what he has; he always wants more. He is always thinking about looting, about destroying countries, about making more weapons. He is always wondering how he can conquer another king. Even when a king's treasury is full, he has no contentment. So as I ate your food, my mind took on that quality of desire, and as a result I stole this necklace. But when I ate the farmer's food, I got diarrhea and all the food I had eaten in your palace was washed out of my body. As the food was washed out, the mental condition that had been derived from it was also erased. I immediately remembered what I had done and came to give the necklace back to you."

The entire being of everyone who handles the food you eat—from the buyer to the cook to the server—goes into that food. Therefore, it is very important that food be cooked and served with the right feeling. For this reason, in our ashram everything from the cooking to the serving is done with respect. The cooks prepare and cook the food with a pure heart, remaining silent and chanting the name of God. While the food is served, everyone chants God's name. In this way, good impressions enter the food and when people eat it they imbibe those good impressions.

The fact is that no matter what kind of food you are eating, if you repeat the name of God before eating it, then it will bear good fruit for you. The name, the mantra, has great power—the power of its own quality. If you eat food with that awareness, then the food will become free of defects. For this reason, in India it is our custom to repeat the name of God while we eat.

We are all created by food. For this reason, we should eat good, pure food, light food that we can digest very quickly and that is appropriate to the season. Mainly, we should eat food with high and sublime feelings. We should kindle the fire of love, devotion, and faith in God so that these feelings are mixed with our food. Then, having that attitude, we should eat that food.

A Good Diet

Q: Is vegetarianism an essential part of spiritual evolution? Will eating small amounts of meat or eggs prevent me from improving my state of consciousness?

SM: I don't care whether you eat a small or a large quantity of meat. I am not an orthodox Hindu; I am interested only in the Truth. Once the president of the International Vegetarian Congress came to visit our ashram in India. He also asked my opinion about eating meat. I told him, "Instead of worrying about my view, I suggest that you perform a very simple experiment. Put a slice of meat on one plate, a slice of fish on another, some eggs on a third plate, and some fruit on a fourth plate. Then look at the plates every two hours and see which food rots first. That will make you understand which foods retain their beauty and fragrance and life energy."

What flesh do those animals eat whose flesh people eat? What meat do those animals eat to fatten themselves? Are they fed meat, or do they eat grass and cereals? If we eat the same thing that they eat, we will also have meat in our bodies. It's not that we have to eat meat to produce meat in our own bodies.

There are very practical reasons for eating vegetarian food. Plants are full of life energy, but there is no life energy in meat. The food we eat is split into three parts during the digestive process. The highest and subtlest portion of it, which is energy itself, becomes one with the *prana*, the life force. The middle portion turns into flesh. The inferior matter becomes waste and is expelled from the system. From meat one gets only the middle portion, which is flesh. One cannot derive any of the life force from it.

I read an interesting statement by the playwright Bernard Shaw. He was a saintly person who had a slim and tall figure. Once someone asked him, "Why don't you eat meat?" Shaw replied, "Do you think my belly is a graveyard, a cemetery in which to bury dead animals?" Shaw was right. I am not talking Hinduism; I am uttering the truth. If meat is so good for us, why are people in the West so fond of salad? It is because they derive the life force from salad.

Milk, butter and cheese, vegetables and fruit, and cereals such as wheat and rice are pure, nourishing, and wholesome and will give you all the energy you need. They contain the essence of food;

they have the life of food, and you will not find this ingredient in eggs, meat, or fish. In America they have discovered that lentils have a lot of protein; in India we call that food *dal*. When I was sick in the hospital, I refused to allow other people to clean my body. Every time the nurses came I refused them. The doctor said, "Let them wash your body." I said, "No, as long as my body does not create a stench, I do not want anybody to wash it." For three and a half weeks I did not allow anyone to wash my body. The doctor told me, "I always wash my body in the morning, but by evening it begins to smell very badly. Why is it that your body does not smell, even though you have not taken a bath for so long?" I said, "Most of the time you eat only stale food that has only bad odors. However, I do not eat that kind of food, so I do not have any stench in my body."

I am not against eating meat; however, I am not in favor of eating meat either. I am seventy-three years old, and so far I have never needed meat to give me energy. I do not feel weak; I have more strength and I am more active than those young people who eat meat. Remember, meat is created from food.

Most of the time you only live by listening to other people and seeing what others do. You do not understand and act for yourself. Wheat, *ghee*, milk, and vegetables are very good for you. If you eat this kind of food, then your body never stinks because that food is very pure.

How to Eat

Q: What is your attitude toward fasting as a spiritual practice?

SM: The body is born of food, it is sustained by food, and in the end it will merge into food. Therefore, it is much better to eat moderately every day than to fast. Eat pure, nourishing food at regular hours, and do not eat between meals. For example, I always eat my lunch between twelve o'clock and twelve thirty. Only between eleven thirty and one o'clock do I feel hungry. When it is time for my lunch, I eat no matter where I am, whether I am in a car or in a plane. Eating is also yoga. If you eat easily digestible, pure, and nourishing food and eat it punctually, then it will be very good for your spiritual growth.

Drugs and Enlightenment

Q: What do you feel about the use of drugs for attaining Self-awareness?

SM: Self-awareness does not depend on anything. But if you take drugs in the name of attaining Self-awareness, you will become dependent on the drugs. Kabir Sahib said, "Never have the hope that you will attain the Self while taking intoxicants." The Self has its own effulgence. The intoxication of drugs is derived from the light of the Self. When this is the case, how can drugs make the light of the Self reveal itself?

A person becomes addicted to drugs, and then to keep himself from admitting this mistake, he says that they give him Self-awareness. When your mind turns within, when you become very, very pure and subtle, the Self reveals itself to you. Every day we chant and meditate and observe good conduct. We do not do these practices to attain the Self, because we have already attained the Self. We do them to make our mind purer and subtler, so that we can perceive the light of the Self. The Self is very subtle, and our mind and intellect must become extremely refined in order to experience it.

If the mind becomes intoxicated and too excited, it becomes rajasic and impure. That is why a person who is addicted to outer intoxicants will find it difficult to experience the intoxication of the inner Self. Meditation affects extremely refined sensory nerves for which drugs are much too strong. These nerves cannot even bear strong coffee. That's why drugs are forbidden by the scriptures.

You should become intoxicated only on God's love. A saint said that a person whose mind has been completely cleansed and whose heart has become pure becomes intoxicated on God's love. And it is the best intoxication. When you get drunk on the intoxication of love for God, all outer drugs will seem insipid by comparison.

Even if you get high on marijuana, you don't get very high, and when the effect wears off, you come down, perhaps even lower than before. To get high again you have to use more marijuana; otherwise, you might not be able to bear your own company. But as you get higher and higher on the intoxicants of the Self, you will reach a state from which you will never come down. So if you want to get high, get high on God's love. You cannot experience this intoxication through drugs.

Meditation is far more potent than marijuana, but before you can get meditation you first have to give up drugs completely. There are no "downs" in meditation; there are only "ups," because the high of meditation will never desert you. It keeps getting stronger and stronger, so powerful is the inner intoxicant. No drug, however potent, can influence a real meditator. It is said that Mira was given poison to drink, yet it caused her no harm for she was under the influence of a far mightier "poison" — the ecstasy and nectar of her love for Krishna. I am not speaking of any miracle or *siddhi*; this happens naturally to one who is divinely intoxicated.

Therefore, meditate with love and interest. Don't seek the aid of drugs; they will dull the refined sensory nerves in your brain. Those who meditate with the aid of drugs always remain insecure and dissatisfied.

The Joy of the Spirit

Q: Is it possible to be a sensual person, to live through one's senses, and at the same time be a spiritual person?

SM: It may be possible; however, it is very difficult to sing and eat at the same time. It is better either to sing or to eat.

Q: I feel that as I look at, hear, and feel the things around me I come closer to the living world, and to me that is very spiritual. But the only way I can do it is through the senses.

SM: That is very good, but what does spirituality mean to you? Spirituality is nothing but an awareness of the fact that the same Truth lives within and without. You can acquire a much better understanding of the outer world by turning within than you can through the senses. I am not suggesting that you should not use the senses. However, the senses perceive only outer, tangible things. Inside, there is a wonder that cannot be perceived by the senses — the wonder of the spirit. True spiritual awareness means seeing matter and Consciousness as one. You cannot have that vision until by turning within and meditating you have experienced Consciousness in its fullness.

Q: In America and other parts of the world we are emerging from the Victorian era. There is now great emphasis on physical freedom. In order to be true to God does one have to keep one's sexuality in check, or can one have sex and still lead a spiritual life?

SM: Why do you have sex? Is it for sensual gratification or for inner peace and fulfillment? Can you say?

Q: Perhaps fulfillment.

SM: But through sex you get only partial fulfillment. Complete and permanent fulfillment is possible only through spiritual practice. If you could experience true inner steadiness even for a moment, your joy would be equal to the joy of a million orgasms. If you could transmute sex into love, you would find that love is thousands of times superior to sex.

I am not against sex, but sexual pleasure is fleeting; according to the scriptures it is as fleeting as a lightning flash. Every kind of creature experiences it, so there is nothing very extraordinary about a human being experiencing it. However, you should be aware of the value of the sexual fluid. The sexual fluid contains the subtle essence of a human body; an entire human body arises from a single drop of sexual fluid, and it grows with the help of the strength that is in the sexual fluid. Once you understand this, you will treat the sexual fluid with reverence. It contains great power. When there is less semen in the body, the mind becomes weak and wanders more. That is why older people are not able to absorb learning as quickly as the young.

The sexual fluid is the source of health, longevity, and endurance. Though I am an old man, because of the retention of sexual fluid I feel very young inside. Sexual fluid is your glow, your vigor, your radiance, and your contentment. It also gives strength to your *prana* and gives force to your meditation. It is the force of the sexual fluid which powers one's meditation. If you were to hold it inside, it would give you tremendous energy and make you much more attractive. As a person conserves the sexual fluid, it begins to move upward in the body. Then he gains tremendous power. Just as you save some of your earnings in the bank, you should save some of your sexual fluid.

I am not against sex—after all, I was also born in that way. I am not suggesting total denial of sex, nor do the scriptures suggest it.

They recommend moderation. In India we make delicacies for special occasions and bring them out only at those times. If you could treat sex in that way, it would be very good.

Sex and Health

Q: Many professional therapists in the West are suggesting that a healthy sexual life is necessary for health and a panacea for most problems. Would you comment on this please?

SM: Small children also get sick. What is the panacea for them? What medicine have the therapists come up with? This is the delusion of reformers. There should be moderation in sex just as there should be moderation in diet. Food is good; a person lives because he eats. However, he can have a healthy body only if he eats moderately. If he overeats, food makes him sick. In the same way, one should be moderate in sexual activity. Sex won't destroy diseases; instead, it can create diseases. If a man or woman discharges too much sexual fluid, then the body becomes weak and useless.

There should be discipline in everything. For example, sleep is very good, but has anyone ever recommended sleeping for fifteen days at a stretch? Instead, people follow discipline in sleeping. They set their alarm clocks and get up.

There is strength in the sexual fluid; if a person lacks sexual fluid in his body, then he won't have enough strength. Look at young students. As long as they haven't wasted their sexual fluid, they are very pure and they have powerful memories. They can study very well. They can play with great energy. Modern artists, singers, dancers, actors, and actresses all feel useless after a few years. They have nothing left within them. This is because of the waste of sexual fluid. You should investigate this matter. If there is a place where people have sex too much, you should find out how many hospitals, doctors, and psychologists are in the vicinity. If there is a place where people follow discipline in having sex, you should find out how many hospitals, doctors, and psychologists are there. You should compare the two.

The saints and sages say, "Perform all your actions, but moderately." There should be discipline in all of your actions.

The Musk Deer

Q: I have heard that a spiritual seeker is not supposed to seek pleasure. Is this true?

SM: A spiritual seeker is after pleasure, but the pleasure he is seeking is not the pleasure of the senses. It is the pleasure of the Self, the bliss of the Self. People chase after sense pleasures because they are not aware of their true nature or of the bliss that is found there. The pleasures of the senses are like the waters of a mirage.

Vedantic philosophy uses the analogy of the musk deer to describe the state we are in. The musk deer emits a very beautiful fragrance from its navel, but the deer thinks that the smell is coming from somewhere outside. So it runs in one direction, searching for the source. Then it senses that the fragrance is coming from somewhere else and runs in the opposite direction. In this way, it constantly searches here and there without knowing that the fragrance is coming from its own body. The more it runs and leaps, the more it smells the fragrance. It thinks, "If I run fast, I'll smell more fragrance." In this way, it constantly wanders in the forest, until at last it collapses and its head falls to its navel. Then for the first time it realizes that the fragrance is arising from within itself.

This is our predicament. The pleasure that we think we get from the senses actually comes from inside us. We keep leaping and running, trying to find it outside. But if we were to become still and turn within, we would experience real bliss.

5

The Inner Attitude

That Is Why You Are What You Are

It is not the actions of other people that give us trouble, but our own nature, our own attitude, and our own actions. This is why we must cultivate virtuous qualities. It is not enough to do *sadhana*. If a person practices yoga religiously but is not equipped with virtuous qualities, then instead of staying on the right path, he may take a wrong turn. When a person falls from virtue, he is seized by difficulties and attachments.

A great being said, "If a person is virtuous, there is no plane where he will not find happiness, no object from which he will not derive joy, and no person who will not appear loving to him." In the *Bhagavad Gita* the virtuous qualities are called divine wealth; in fact, it is said that these are the only true wealth. This is the wealth you should try to attain, because only this wealth will stay with you. It does not matter how intelligent or accomplished you are, because if you lack virtues your other qualities will not help you in the end.

In India there was a great scholar named Vaman Pandit. He had attained the highest degree, because with his knowledge he had defeated India's best scholars in debate seven times. However, he was very arrogant and always looked down on others. Eventually, he decided to go to Benares, to Kashi, in order to conquer the great scholars there. (Benares is the greatest center of learning in India. No one has ever defeated the scholars of Benares.)

One night during his journey he was sitting by a river under an *ashwatthama* tree, when he heard loud voices coming from the branches overhead. He looked up and saw two *brahmarakshasas*

99

(demons) sitting on a branch of the tree quarreling loudly. One of them said, "Don't you sit there," and the other said, "Don't you sit there." One of them asked, "Why shouldn't I sit here?" The other replied, "You defeated everybody only four times, and I conquered everybody five times. However, the man who is sitting under this tree has conquered all the scholars *seven* times, so we should really reserve a good place for him."

The scholar was surprised when he heard this. He thought, "Even after defeating everybody so many times am I only to become a demon like them?" He gave up his ambition to defeat any more scholars and got rid of his arrogance and pride. After that, he became a truly great scholar and wrote a very beautiful commentary on the *Bhagavad Gita*, the *Bhagavat Dipika*.

The fact is that none of your talents and none of your skills are of any real value compared to your wealth of virtue. No matter where you go, you carry your faults and virtues with you, and it is these that determine your state. It is when a person falls from virtue and good conduct that he is seized with difficulties and ailments.

In the Indian scriptures this world of ours is called *karmabhumi*, the land of action, because this is the plane where we perform actions, good or bad, for which we receive good or bad fruits. No matter what actions we perform in this world, we receive their fruits. For this reason, we should always keep an account of ourselves. We should not try to keep track of others, of how many sins others have committed, how many mistakes they have made, or how much more advanced they are than we. Instead, we should always remember what we have done and what we have to do in the future. We should check to see how much self-control we have developed, how much equanimity there is in our minds, how much steadfastness we have achieved. We should check to see how much we have been able to rid ourselves of our desires, our anger, our jealousy, and our tendency to hate other people, to rejoice at their misfortune, to feel sad when we see them advance. We should see how much compassion we have acquired, how much we have learned to love honesty and truthfulness, how loving we have become. We should always be aware of our faults and always try to increase our virtuous qualities. Above all, we should check our attitude. It is our inner attitude and feeling that determine our behavior. Not only that, it is these that determine our experience of the world.

In the *Yoga Vasishtha* there is a great and mysterious statement: "The world is as you see it." Whatever feeling you have within you is the feeling you will project onto the world. Therefore, according to your own vision, the world becomes good or bad, pleasurable or painful, a storehouse of happiness or a mine of sorrow. It is your own attitude that bears fruit for you and makes you who you are.

In India there was an intoxicated being who always used to say the same thing: "That's why you are what you are." In God's creation there are two types of people. One type will give something to another person, while the other type will snatch something away. Sometimes someone would give this great being a piece of bread, and sometimes someone else would take it away. This disparity is God's creation. But no matter what happened, this ecstatic being would always say, "That's why you are what you are." If there is somebody who praises you, there is also somebody else who blames you. That is why the saint always said, "That's why you are what you are."

One day when the saint was in an intoxicated mood, he entered the palace of a great king. At the first gate stood two guards holding spears. They seized him rudely and asked him where he thought he was going. He said, "That's why you are what you are," slipped past them, and went inside.

The king's prime minister happened to be standing nearby and was interested by what he saw, so he began to follow the saint. At the second gate a guard stopped the saint with a pistol. The saint said, "That's why you are what you are." He went farther and came across another guard, who held a higher position. The only thing that this guard said was, "Stop! Don't go inside!" The saint replied, "That's why you are what you are." He went farther inside, and there he was met by the officer of the guards, who said, "O Babaji, come here. Where are you going?"

"I want to meet the king."

"Fine," said the officer, "but take care of yourself."

"That's why you are what you are," said the saint. He went farther until he met the chief of police. The chief came forward and asked him politely, "Where are you going?"

"Inside."

"All right, you may go inside."

"That's why you are what you are."

Then the saint went farther. The next person he met was the prime minister, who had hurried to arrive ahead of him. The prime minister asked, "Where do you want to go?"

"To the king."

"Come with me. I will take you."

"That's why you are what you are," said the saint. When the king saw the saint, he immediately stepped down from his throne and brought a chair for him to sit on. At this the saint said, "That's why you are what you are."

Now the prime minister asked, "O Babaji, will you clarify something for me? I have been following and watching you all this time. Whenever the guards stopped you, you said, 'That's why you are what you are.' No matter what was said or done to you, all that you said was, 'That's why you are what you are.' Will you please explain to me the meaning of this statement?"

"It's very simple," said the saint. "That's why you are what you are."

"But what's the mystery?"

"The mystery is this. The value a person gives to others depends on his own worthiness. Whatever attitude he has, that is how he sees, and that is how he behaves."

The prime minister asked, "What do you mean?"

"The guards at the front door had little understanding. That's why they are what they are. Look at them. They stay at the front door, far away from the palace, and receive only a small salary. The guard at the next gate has a slightly higher position. Still, he stopped me with a pistol. He had that much understanding, so that's why he is what he is. The third guard told me, 'Stop!' He had a little more understanding; that's why he is what he is. The fourth guard asked me, 'O Babaji, where are you going?' That's why he is what he is. He is a big officer. The chief of police had more brains and a higher position. Therefore, he came forward and asked me, 'Where do you want to go?' That's why he is what he is. As I went farther I came across you, the prime minister, who received me with great respect and brought me to the king. That's why you are what you are; you work under the king and take care of everything in the kingdom. Then I met the king. The moment he saw me he stood up and offered me a chair. He asked me how I was and was very loving and hospitable. And that is why he is what he is."

People become what they are according to the attitude they hold in their mind, and that attitude is what they project onto the world. Whatever worth you yourself have, you project that around you, and that is what you see. Therefore, if you want to become very worthy, it is important to cultivate a high attitude, an attitude of purity and divinity. Above all else, it is your attitude that bears fruit for you. You become what you become according to your own feeling and your own attitude. Many religious people take the attitude that a human being is a sinful creature, that he is a mine of bad qualities which have to be purified. But if a person looks upon himself as sinful, he ensures that he will commit sinful actions. If you think of yourself as a sinner, it will not be long before you say to yourself, "Since I am a sinner anyway, why shouldn't I commit one more bad action?"

But if you understand that your innermost being is totally pure, if you identify yourself with that purity and know that that is who you are, you will not want to commit bad actions; you will not want to sully that purity. If you look at yourself with great love and respect, understanding that divinity dwells within you, then automatically, in the course of time, good qualities will begin to manifest in you. Whether you are in the world or in spiritual life, whether you are a businessman, an artist, or a worker, the root of everything is faith in the Self. Whoever has attained faith in the Self has attained everything. Everyone respects people who have faith in the Self. Of course, wealth respects such people, but even mishaps respect such people.

The truth is that the worst sin, the root of all sins, is to insult or belittle your own Self, while the greatest of all virtues is to respect the Self. It does not matter if the world insults you, but you should not insult your own Self. "What theft has that person not committed who has stolen the glory from the Self?" a great being said. Therefore, keep respecting yourself. To look upon yourself as low, as petty, as small, to see yourself as sinful or bad is to deny the great divinity within you. When you look upon yourself with a low attitude, you will also see the world with that attitude. You will project your own feeling onto others, and then you will see in them the same wretchedness you see in yourself. Then you will begin to find faults in other people, to look at them with the eye of sin, and to discover impurities in everything around you. Therefore, first of all you should understand your own greatness and your own divinity. Then you will understand the divinity in others. Once you begin to realize that God Himself dwells within the human heart, once you begin to respect yourself, you will automatically respect others. Then you will begin to see that the world is very beautiful, and you will behave very beautifully with others.

Every good thing flows from this attitude of respect. For this reason, the most important action you can perform is to welcome yourself and others with respect and love. Kabir said, "In every heart. God dwells perfectly, in His fullness. Therefore, do not use harsh words, do not speak bitterly to others, because your beloved is sitting within." The great sage Kapilamuni told his mother, "If a person insults that God who lives within other human beings and then goes to a temple and prays to an idol of God, will God be pleased with him?" The greatest virtue, the highest action, and the best form of worship is to look upon other people with the awareness that the Self is in all.

It is only because people lack this feeling of the Self in others that so many bad things are happening in this world. Because people do not see the Self in others there are fights between husband and wife, between parents and children, between parties in society. The reason for all these things is lack of respect for the Self. A person who sees truly sees that no person, creature, or object is apart from him. For such a person, there is no difference between sentient and insentient objects. There is no such thing as beautiful and ugly. There is no feeling of high and low. For such a person there is only equality in this universe, and all the virtuous qualities come to him. Only a person who sees with this attitude can be called a virtuous person, a high person, a great person.

How to Become Pure

Q: If one has become impure, what is the fastest and best way to purify oneself? Does living with the Guru make one pure more quickly than performing austerities?

SM: To live with the Guru is the greatest austerity. It is very difficult. You should not merely live in the physical presence of the Guru. You should absorb his teachings. If you learn how to be with the

Guru, it will be very good. If you are with the Guru even for a moment, it will last for your entire life. Tulsidas was a great saint who said, "If you are with the Guru, a saint, or a great being even for twenty minutes, or if not twenty minutes then for ten, or if not for ten then for five, or even if you can be with him only for a minute or a fraction of a moment, then all the sins of your countless lives are destroyed. You can reform yourself."

But the real question is, In what way does a person think that he has become impure? Does he think that he has become impure because he has not taken a bath or because his clothes are dirty? We have this defect of thinking that we are impure, but this is not right. It has become traditional to say, "I am a sinner, I am a sinner. I am worthless. I am no good at all." But what is it that is a sinner? Is the body a sinner? Is the Self a sinner? A poet-saint said, "If you look at this body, you will see that it is made of seven elements. There is no eighth element." If you look at the Self, you will see that the Self is only one. Not only that, the Self is full of knowledge and purity. No fault can ever come close to the Self. Nothing can taint the Self. So where does the impurity lie? It is neither in the body nor in the Self. Therefore, you should come to the conclusion that impurity lies in a person's lack of understanding. You should improve your understanding. Your present understanding can be dangerous for you.

When I was young and had just received *sannyasa* initiation, I went to Allahabad, to the place where the three holy rivers Ganga, Jamuna, and Saraswati converge. I had just taken a bath in the river and was sitting on its bank. A priest came to me and told me, "Now make a resolution, make a resolution."

I said, "I have just taken *sannyasa* initiation; I have given up all my desires, so I am completely pure. I have also worshipped God by taking a dip in the river, and it is said that a person who bathes in the Ganga becomes totally free of sins. So I have become very pure, and that is true worship of God."

However, the priest wanted me to perform another kind of worship. Before he arrived I had been extremely happy, but he kept pestering me. He had brought all the articles that were needed for worship, and he would not leave me alone. He wanted me to worship God with his *puja* articles, not for my own benefit, but because if I did the worship I would have to pay him one and a half rupees. I thought, "If I perform this worship, at least he will leave me alone." So I agreed to perform the worship.

"Now I will repeat some mantras," he said, "and you repeat them after me." Then he began to repeat his mantras. They were "I am a sinner, I was born of sins, and I perform sinful actions." When I heard them, I said, "I'm not going to repeat these mantras. I am not a sinner; you are the one who is a sinner." Immediately the priest dropped his *puja* articles and took off.

It is from people like this that you learn the wrong understanding about yourself. You learn that you are sinful; you learn that you are bad. You never learn that you are beautiful or that God dwells inside you. So where does your impurity lie? In your Self? In your body? Where? Discard this feeling of impurity because it hinders your spiritual progress. It makes you dependent and becomes a barrier to your unfoldment. Therefore, give up your feeling of being a sinner. Even if you have committed bad actions in the past, you should not dwell on them. You should not think that you have become impure because of them. Once a devotee of my Baba came to him and complained about another devotee. "That man drinks liquor and eats fish," he told Baba.

"So what?" Baba said. "No matter what he eats or drinks, he shits it out the next day. He doesn't hang onto it, so why should you?" No matter what you may have done in the past, you should let go of it. If the thought "I am a sinner" arises then have another thought: "I am not a sinner. I am meritorious."

The Upanishads say that a person is what he thinks. Whatever he thinks is what he becomes. So why have painful and wretched thoughts about yourself? Why not have sublime and great thoughts?

Honoring Yourself

Q: How can I honor and love myself when I see so many faults in myself?

SM: You should make a point of honoring yourself for a certain period every day, and while honoring yourself you should forget about your faults. I may feel angry this evening, but when I sit for meditation the next morning there should be no trace of that anger left in me. Then I can honor myself and meditate. Just as during sleep you only sleep and do nothing else, similarly while honoring yourself you should only honor yourself. You should not do anything else. In the course of time you will begin to honor yourself for longer and longer periods.

You should lose consciousness of your weakness. Attachment and aversion may be there, but along with them there are also many good qualities. You may not honor yourself for your faults, but you can certainly honor yourself for your good qualities.

Don't underrate yourself. Don't let your price fall on the market by keeping the memory of all your faults, attachments, and aversions alive. Depending on your temperament, attachment and aversion will persist for quite some time. You should keep cultivating and developing good qualities. Do not let the consciousness of your attachments and hatreds become constant. Hatred and attachment do not last, so why should your consciousness of them last? The sign of a wise person is that if something undesirable takes place in his life, he forgets about it very quickly.

The Awareness of Equality

You can meditate, you can do yoga, you can perform austerities, but as long as you haven't attained equal vision none of these practices will show you God.

There was a being called Namdev before whom the Lord used to manifest, singing and dancing. Namdev was a popular saint. Because God was physically with him, he had the complete knowledge of God as form. But he did not know God in His formless, all-pervasive aspect. If a wise person wants to teach something to one of his own family members, then he always sends him away to another teacher. In the same way, when the Lord wanted to teach Namdev, He sent him away. One day the Lord said, "Namdev, you should go to Pandharpur. There are many great beings there, many great saints." In India there are many, many holy places, one of which is Pandharpur. At that time there were many Siddhas, perfected beings, from every walk of life who used to gather in Pandharpur in the month of Ashad, which corresponds to July.

Namdev agreed with great pleasure to go and meet the saints. He went to Pandharpur, and when he arrived he saw the main saints sitting in a group. They were all great; even the Lord had praised their glory. Namdev saw that they were all having a discussion, and he too sat down.

There is a custom that you must follow in India when you are in front of an audience. To show your respect, you must lower your head, you must bow before you enter. It doesn't matter to which temple you go, it doesn't matter to which society the temple belongs, but when you enter a temple, when you enter a holy place, you must bow to show the respect that you feel.

When Namdev arrived, he just looked at the saints. He neither bowed to them nor offered them his salutations. He had a lot of pride because of his personal relationship with God. According to Namdev, every sage was very small compared with him, because he thought that he alone was with God. All the saints kept quiet and looked at him.

Jnaneshwar Maharaj was in the gathering. He was a very intelligent Guru, a very intelligent saint. Although he was very young in age, he was great. When he was sixteen years old, he wrote a commentary on the *Bhagavad Gita*. Before he began his work, Jnaneshwar Maharaj always said, "O my own Self who pervades everything and everybody, I offer my salutations to you." Once some doubting brahmin priests pointed to a buffalo and asked him, "Is the Self in this buffalo, too?" Jnaneshwar said, "Certainly." They asked, "Then can this buffalo recite the Vedas?" Jnaneshwar Maharaj addressed the buffalo, saying, "O Narayan, recite the Vedas!" The buffalo began to recite in Sanskrit. It wasn't a miracle that Jnaneshwar performed; it was the power of the Self that made it happen. When you have the awareness that all is the Self, the power of the Self is yours.

In the group there was another saint who was old and who used to make pots. Pointing at Namdev, Jnaneshwar asked the potter, "O uncle, how is that pot? Is it baked or unbaked?" The potter had a thick stick with which he tested whether a pot was baked or unbaked. So he took the stick and began to hit everybody's head — tum, tum, tum. When he came to Namdev he also hit his head. Namdev was enraged. He said, "What is this? You are insulting a devotee. I am the friend of Panduranga, God."

Every saint said, "Kick him out of here. That pot is unbaked; it is not ripe." Namdev was completely insulted. He said to himself, "I am God's friend, yet they tell me that I am an idiot. They are kicking me out."

Who isn't with God? God is within you and within me. God is within and God is without. Why should it be that only Namdev had God? We, too, have God. Whether you know it or not, whether you accept it or not, God is with everyone.

A great being teaches in strange and unique ways. The medicine that he gives each devotee for his ego is unique; only a great being knows what medicine you need.

Namdev got up with great anger and left in a huff. He went back to the Lord and began to speak to Him very angrily. "That company wasn't very good. They hit my head; they told me I was unbaked, and they told me to get out."

The Lord said, "You know, that is absolutely true."

"What?" Namdev said. "It's true? I'm unbaked?"

"Absolutely. You haven't yet attained any knowledge of God."

"But You are right before me," Namdev said. "I am speaking to You, Lord."

The Lord said, "Just by knowing My form you are not going to know who God is."

It is said that as long as you don't have equal awareness, equal vision, your meditation and knowledge are useless. Shaivism says, "Everything is the play of Consciousness, the play of the power of God." As long as you do not have this knowledge, you will not attain anything. However, a being who has this awareness attains God and sees God. A great being said, "If a person attains a god who is restricted to only one place, to only one size, then he is not even doing *sadhana*. He is not even a seeker. He is not even close to doing *sadhana* or to being a seeker. On the other hand, when a person becomes aware that God lives in everything and is everywhere, without restrictions, then he is the best among seekers. He is not merely a seeker, but a *yogi raja*, a king among yogis."

Namdev asked, "O Lord, what do You want me to do now?"

The Lord said, "This is not My work."

Namdev asked, "Who will bake me then?"

The Lord told Namdev to go and receive instructions from Visoba

Khechara, a saint in Alandi. In Alandi, behind Jnaneshwar Maharaj's *samadhi* shrine, there is a beautiful Shiva temple. Namdev went there and asked the townspeople, "Where does Visoba Khechara live?" They replied, "He is inside the Shiva temple, the Mahadev temple."

Visoba Khechara was an old man. He wore a turban around his head and shoes on his feet. He was ecstatic. He was lying down, snoring. Both of his feet were on top of the *lingam*. When Namdev went inside and saw this scene, he did not feel good at all. How could this person give Namdev instructions when he himself put his shoes and feet on the head of God, on the *lingam*? He said to himself, "Alas! I have lost my path. First the Lord sent me to a place where I got a blow on the head, and now He sends me here. This is worse than before! Where have I come?"

Nonetheless, he thought, "At least I can help him to put his feet on the floor." Like many people, he had the delusion of trying to earn merit by helping others, by being compassionate and doing social work. People do not realize that while trying to help others they themselves are going downhill.

Namdev went inside, tapped the wall, and asked, "O noble man, how are you sleeping? Where are you putting your feet?"

Visoba Khechara opened his eyes and said, "O brother, what are you saying?"

Namdev replied, "Don't you understand that you have put your feet on God! You are asking me what I am saying? Please put your feet down."

Visoba Khechara said, "Why don't you remove my feet? Look, I am an old man. You want to help me out. You have a lot of compassion in your heart. I am so old, my legs are so weak, that I can't really put them anywhere. Will you help? Put my feet where there is no *lingam*."

Because Namdev had an addiction to social work, he was delighted to oblige. He took both of Visoba Khechara's feet, lifted them, and tried to put them on the floor. The same *shivalingam* followed his feet. Once again he took the feet and tried to place them elsewhere. Once again the *lingam* followed the feet. Wherever he tried to put the feet there appeared a *lingam*. At last he realized what was happening and he held onto the feet. He said, "The Lord sent me to you to receive instructions from you. Please give me some instructions."

Visoba Khechara recited two poems for Namdev. He said, "God exists in every atom; He fills every particle of dust. Do you realize that? Don't think that God is in one place. He is everywhere." Then he said, "God dwells not just in a temple, not just in Vaikuntha, but in every pore of your body. The Vedas say that He is limitless, ancient, invisible. The eyes cannot perceive Him. However, in the heart of a noble person who knows Him, the same One exists. He permeates every pore of his body."

Khechara said, "O Namdev, whatever you can see, whatever you cannot see, is God. Now go." At that moment Namdev attained the knowledge of That.

So enlightenment is wisdom, equal awareness. The Lord said, "O Arjuna, as long as you don't have equal awareness, you can't know Him; you can't attain Him."

The Quality of Humility

Everything in this universe practices equality-consciousness. The earth is the same everywhere. The earth of India does not say, "Only Indians can walk on me." The air is the same everywhere. The air over America does not say, "I belong to America so you cannot breathe me." Water is the same everywhere. If you mix water from India with water from England, it will still be water. The sun is the same everywhere. It does not say, "This person is good so I will shine on him, and that person is bad so I will leave him in darkness." Only human beings make distinctions among people, among objects, and among countries. Yet a true human being is one who regards all with the same awareness, understanding that God dwells in everything equally.

Tukaram Maharaj, the great saint of Maharashtra, sang in one of his poems, "O Lord, I am going to worship You in this way. I will offer my salutations to whatever exists, as though it were You." This is the essence of equality-awareness. Like Tukaram, a person who sees everything with true equality-awareness becomes very humble. He bows down in worship before everyone, understanding that everyone is the form of God. For this reason, it is said that humility is one of the divine virtues. It is very great; it is one of the qualities of God.

Once the Pandavas, who were great kings, held a big *yajna*, or fire ritual. Many kings and princes attended, and one of them was Lord Krishna, an incarnation of God. Each of the kings and princes was given a particular task to perform. One was put in charge of taking care of the guests, another saw to the provisioning of the animals, and so on. Everyone had an important role. When Krishna was asked which job he would do, he said, "I will take the job of picking up the leaf plates after the feast." This is humility. Humility is not meant only for people who are without intelligence, talents, or energy. It is a quality that arises naturally in a person who has begun to be aware of his identity with God. Just as a wealthy person's wealth is reflected in his manner and bearing, when a person has attained divine wealth, it manifests itself in humility.

It is only through humility that a person can go close to God. A person who understands God understands that any form of pride — whether it is the pride of status or the pride of wealth or the pride of intellect — is nothing before God. That is why one of the great saints sang, "O Lord, take away the pride of my mind. Take away the cleverness of my intellect. Make me as humble as a village dog." Being humble does not mean being weak or meek. A humble person may appear to be very mild, but in reality he has immense strength. Tukaram says in one of his poems, "We servants of Vishnu are softer than cotton, but we can break a thunderbolt." Humility has great power. A sage said that when a person has true humility, even fire becomes a small puddle in front of him. A lion becomes like a small cat in his presence. Before him, a mountain becomes nothing but a stone. A person who is truly humble conquers all.

Give Up Pride

There is as much love inside us as there is in God, but we never reach that center within. To experience this abundance of love we have to be very clean and very clear. I do not mean the physical cleanliness that comes when we take a shower and put on makeup and newly pressed clothes. I mean having a clean heart, a pure heart. Having a clean heart means not allowing oneself to create faults inside. It also means not seeing others' faults.

An aphorism in Narada's *Bhakti Sutras* is "The only blocks to the rise of love are pride and pretension." We cling to our pride and pretension, but truly they are the source of our failure. They hide the Truth, they suppress love, and they create constant agitation so that we always find ourselves living in unhappiness.

Once there was a person who had a great desire to attain God but who was blocked. He had passed through countless lifetimes and was filled with countless impressions of pride and pretension. This seeker went to a Guru and said, "I want to follow the path to God. Please initiate me."

The Guru replied, "Go and take a bath in the river, and then come back." In India before a seeker receives initiation, he must take a bath as part of a ritual of purification. The seeker went off to bathe.

In the meantime the great being called a sweeper and said, "A man will be coming here very soon. The moment you see him, start sweeping and make dust fly in the air." When the sweeper saw the seeker, she began to sweep very fast so that dust flew all over him.

In India at that time there was a caste system, and sweepers were looked down upon and regarded as impure. When the dirt flew all over the seeker, he became furious. "What's the matter with you?" he shouted. "Couldn't you see me coming? I just took a bath and I am so pure, but now you are getting dust all over me!" He was ready to beat the sweeper, but he controlled his temper, brushed himself off, and entered the ashram. When the Guru saw him, he said, "You haven't become clean. Come back in a year when you have become clean."

The seeker left, and returned one year later. Once again the Guru said to him, "Go and take a bath." Then he called the sweeper and told her, "Fill a basket with garbage and hold it on your head. The moment the seeker comes close to you, bump into him so that the basket of garbage falls all over him."

As soon as the sweeper saw the man coming back from his bath, she bumped into him and the entire basket fell on his head. A year ago this man had almost beat the sweeper. This time he had no desire to beat her, but he was still very irritated.

When he entered the ashram, the teacher said, "You are still filthy. Go away and become clean, and then come back in a year."

The seeker left, and a year later came to the Guru for the third time. Again the Guru said, "Go and take a bath." Then he told the sweeper, "This time, if he says anything to you while you are sweeping, hit him twice with the broom."

When the seeker returned from his bath, the woman was sweeping. He said, "Move aside." The sweeper turned the broom upside down and gave him four blows. The Guru had told her to give him two blows, but she had her own ax to grind. This time the seeker received the blows without saying anything. When he went inside, the Guru said, "Now you can sit down. You are ready to receive something."

If you want to experience love, first of all give up pride and then give up the pretensions that follow pride.

The Queen's Bed

Q: How can I stop comparing myself with others and remain contented with my life situation?

SM: You don't seem to have any sense in your head. Why should you go around comparing yourself with others? Why don't you try to attain awareness of the inner Self, which is the creator of all, and become anchored in that awareness? If there is anything you should compare yourself with, it is your own inner Self, your own Consciousness. Only then will you attain stability.

There is no purpose in looking at others, comparing oneself with others, or envying others. The inner state of all beings, from a small creature to a millionaire, is the same. Only on the surface does it appear as though everyone is different.

Once a maid was making a queen's bed. The bed was very beautiful, and the maid thought, "This bed is so soft! How well the queen must sleep!" Just to give it a try, she lay down on the bed, and the moment she put her head on the pillow she fell asleep. Just then, the queen entered the room. Now, the queen was full of the pride of her own authority, and she was outraged by the sight of her servant sleeping in her bed. She got a whip and gave the maid several blows. Immediately the maid woke up and cried out,

"Alas, alas!" but the queen would not stop beating her. She was under the control of her anger, and she had completely lost her discrimination. But as the queen was beating the maid, something strange happened. The maid began to laugh. This puzzled the queen so much that she put down her whip. While the maid had been screaming and weeping, the queen had continued to beat her; it was only when she began to laugh that the blows stopped. In the same way, if we become satisfied with whatever we receive, understanding that it is the gift of God, then immediately we will start experiencing joy instead of unhappiness.

The queen said to her maid, "When I began to beat you, you cried, but then your tears turned to laughter. What happened?"

The maid replied, "At first I cried because the blows were so painful. Then a great awareness dawned on me. I realized that if I received so many blows after sleeping in this bed for only a few minutes, how many blows must you receive when you sleep here all the time!"

Like the maid, you should have right understanding. Do not be envious of the wealth or position of others. You never know how many blows are hiding behind them. You should have satisfaction in your heart. The *Bhagavad Gita* says that only a person who is satisfied with whatever he has, who has transcended the pairs of opposites, who faces everything with an equal awareness can become supremely happy. The only true happiness comes from the wisdom of the Self. It is foolish to look at others. Why don't you look at your own Self?

The Maid Who Let Go of the Carrot

Once there was a maid who worked in the house of a rich man. One day a *sadhu* came to the door asking for food, and the maid took a carrot from her master's kitchen and gave it to him. It was the one charitable action of her life.

Time passed, and the maid died. She was taken to the visa office of the next world, where the officials checked her file. They saw that she had performed one charitable action, and for this they decided she should enjoy three months in heaven. Because she had given away a carrot, they handed her an enormous carrot and told her, "Hold onto this carrot and it will take you to heaven."

Many people were standing in the visa office waiting for their cases to be decided. They saw the maid grab hold of the carrot and watched it rise. They knew that the carrot was going to heaven, and they thought that if they went along they would escape their own judgment. First one man grabbed the maid's feet. Another man grabbed his feet. Then another person grabbed the second man's feet. Soon, one hundred people were holding on. The carrot kept going higher, until the maid could see heaven right before her eyes. Only a small distance was left before she would be at the gate.

At that moment the maid looked down to find out how far she had come. When she saw so many people holding onto her feet, she was furious! "You rascals!" she cried. "You idiots! Holding onto my feet! I performed the charitable action, and you are taking advantage of it! Leave my feet alone!" She began to shoo them away with her hands. Of course, when she did that, she let go of the carrot. The carrot went higher, but she fell to the ground and everyone else fell along with her. Some broke their backs, some broke their legs, some broke their heads, and nobody went to heaven.

Why did this happen? Simply because of one person's jealousy. Why did the maid become so upset? What did it matter if a hundred people went with her to heaven? Isn't heaven big enough for everyone? So be very vigilant. Stay away from negative feelings. Do not let yourself burn in jealousy and anger. They will make you fall.

Praise and Blame

Once Saint Makarios was approached by a few spiritual seekers who asked him to instruct them on spiritual matters. He told them to go to the cemetery and to abuse the people buried there using all sorts of vile language. The seekers did as Makarios instructed, then returned to him. The following day Makarios sent them back to the cemetery with the instructions that they should praise all the people buried there with the most eloquent language. The seekers were amazed by Makarios's instructions. Nonetheless, they followed them perfectly, saying to each of the corpses, "You are so great and

sublime. Your father and forefathers were so great and sublime."
When they returned to Makarios, he asked them, "What was the
reaction of those dead people when you abused them?"

They said, "Nobody uttered even a single word."

"And when you praised them today, what was their reaction?"

"Today, too, nobody uttered a single word," they said.

"This is my instruction to you," said Makarios. "Like those corpses,
try to look at praise and censure with equal-mindedness."

A seeker should try to go beyond praise and blame. If people
criticize you, what harm will you get from it? If people praise you,
what good will it do you? Suppose a news item appeared in one of
the newspapers saying that I was a very great Siddha Guru. If I
were bound within, what good would the praise of the newspapers
do me? Or suppose certain people were to abuse me, saying that I
was imperfect and had no knowledge? If I were not imperfect, what
harm could their words do me? There is not much meaning in
receiving praise or censure from other people. A saint sang, "Try to
develop your awareness or understanding. Try to elevate yourself,
to make yourself the supreme God Himself." Praise and insults are
like thorns that get stuck in your feet. Do not attach much importance
to them; instead, try to become established in your own being.

There was a great saint called Siddharudha Swami. *Arudha* means
"one who is permanently established in his own Self." When I was
young, I lived in his ashram. Thousands of people used to chant
there continuously, and he used to feed many, many people every
day. He was a very great and charitable soul. One day some
wandering *sadhus* came to the ashram. They insisted that the swami
give them money so that they could buy *ganja*, marijuana. The
swami said, "You can take food here, but I won't give you money
for marijuana." Because Siddharudha refused to give them money,
the *sadhus* started abusing him. One of them used very harsh
language; he said, "You bastard, I will hump your wife." Half a
dozen of Siddharudha's devotees were standing around, and when
they heard the *sadhu* abuse their Guru, they grabbed him and were
about to beat him. Siddharudha Swami said, "Wait a minute. What
blunder has this man committed that you are so angry with him?"

"Didn't you hear his harsh language?" the disciples asked. "We
cannot tolerate it. He has said that he will hump your wife."

Then Siddharudha said, "You are forgetting one thing. I am a lifelong celibate; I never married! They threatened to abuse a wife I do not even have! So how can their words harm me?"

If someone abuses you, you have to use your power of discrimination. First, think whether you deserve this criticism. If you do, then change yourself. If you do not, then why should you accept it? There is no value in praise or censure for a person on the spiritual path. If we want to make real progress, then we have to transcend this pair of opposites. We remain unhappy because we are bound by these dualities; we are affected by praise and censure. To transcend them is not the instruction of just one or two saints; it is the recommendation of all the saints who have ever lived. All the saints have insisted that one should go beyond praise and censure and also that one should not praise or blame others.

Kabir says in one of his poems: Let others fight, but you keep remembering God. When the elephant sways in its own ecstasy, the dogs begin to bark at him, but the elephant leaves the dogs alone. In the same way, you should keep remembering the Lord continually, and if others want to fight, let them. All sorts of words are written on blank pieces of paper. Let those who are interested in such things read them—you should just keep remembering the Lord.

Overcoming Fear

Q: How can I overcome fear?

SM: To a certain extent, fear is after everyone. Within the heart, there is a center of fear, just as there is a center of greed, a center of desire, and a center of ignorance. A great sage sang that there is no one in this world who is not subject to fear. A person who is enjoying pleasures is afraid of disease. A person who holds a high position is afraid of falling. A scholar is afraid of competition from other scholars. A wealthy person is afraid of a king. A king is afraid of his enemies. And everyone is afraid of old age and death. Only the inner Self is completely free of fear. Nonetheless, there is absolutely no need for fear. You experience fear only as long as you do not know the inner Self and are not aware of its immense power.

Only a person who believes that he is different from the Self, that he is other than the Self, who maintains his separate identity as a man or a woman, remains fearful. Fear exists in the feeling of separation, the feeling of otherness. The moment you acquire knowledge of the Truth, you will become fearless. Yet even if you do not have knowledge of the Self, you should realize that there is nothing to be afraid of. You should never be afraid of death or of sickness. You should never wonder what is going to happen. Instead, you should trust God. Understand that you are the Self. Understand that the Guru's Shakti always stands behind you. Understand that God and Guru exist everywhere: before you, behind you, above you, and below you.

Once there was a famine in Baghdad. The situation was so bad that people were being sold in the market as food. A priest was walking down the road, when he saw a slave standing by the roadside. The slave looked very joyful, as if he did not care about anything.

"O slave," the priest asked, "how is it that you are so happy? There is famine in Baghdad, and people are eating one another. Why do you look so happy?"

The slave replied, "I have a great master, the master of the world. He can fulfill all of my desires. When this is the case, why should I worry?"

Just then the priest heard a voice from above saying, "O priest, you should be ashamed. Even that slave is happy with the understanding that I can take care of him!"

In the same way, you should always trust God. The inner Self exists inside you. God's power, the Guru's power, exists in your body. A person becomes afraid when he feels that he is alone and that no one is taking care of him, but when the Self pervades everywhere, how can anyone ever be alone?

The great saint Kabir said, "O Kabir, why do you wander here and there? Why do you feel that you are an orphan? With a pure mind, meditate on the inner Self. The moment you call Him, He will respond to you." You, too, should have trust in this assurance. It is not only in spiritual life that you should have faith; in worldly life, too, you should have full trust in God. God truly takes care of everything.

In the *Bhagavad Gita*, there is a verse in which the Lord says, "When someone is devoted to Me, I take care of what he already has and secure what he does not possess." There was a great sage who used to read the *Gita* every day. He had full trust in the Lord. At one point his financial affairs became so bad that he had trouble getting even a single *chapati*. One day his wife cried, "What are we going to do? There's no flour or oil in the house!" The sage comforted her as best he could and then left the house as usual. He went to the bank of the Ganga and began to read the *Gita*. He was reading the chapter in which this verse appears. When he saw the verse, he stopped reading and began to think about whether it was true. After all, writers make mistakes, publishers make mistakes, editors make mistakes. This is what has happened to all the scriptures; the editors have put in their own things, and therefore you can no longer find the original scriptures. The sage thought about this verse for a long time; then he underlined it with a pen to remind himself to think about it more and went on reading the *Gita*.

In the meantime his wife was sitting at home, when she heard a knock at the door. She opened it and saw a beautiful, radiant boy standing there. His arms were full of bags of grain, vegetables, and other things. "These are for you," he said.

The wife was very surprised. "Who sent these?" she asked the boy.

"The *maharaj* who is reading the *Gita* on the bank of the Ganga," he replied.

The wife took the bags inside and offered the boy a glass of water, but then she saw that he had been stabbed and that he was bleeding. "What happened?" she asked. "Who stabbed you?"

"The same scholar, your husband, did this," the boy said.

The wife was shocked and bewildered. She closed her eyes and cried, "Alas! How could he do such a thing?" When she opened her eyes, the boy had disappeared, but she felt such love, peace, and contentment that she fell to the ground, unconscious. When she regained consciousness, she saw that there were many things in the bags, so she began to prepare a meal.

The scholar always read the *Gita* until noon, and afterward, when he returned home, he would eat whatever was there. On this day he walked home very slowly, because in the morning his wife had told him that she did not have any food in the house. As he got closer to the house he began to smell the fragrance of food. He went in and asked his wife, "What are you doing?"

"I have been preparing food since morning," said the wife. "I have already prepared the *puris, seera*, and *pakoras.*"

"Who brought all these things?" he asked.

"A beautiful boy. He brought enough to last for a long time."

"Who was the boy?" asked the scholar.

"The same boy that you stabbed. He told me that you were sitting on the bank of the Ganga and that you had stabbed him."

The sage remembered that he had underlined a verse in the *Gita* with a pen. He realized that it had been God Himself who had come to the house and that it had been his lack of faith in the truth of the verse that had caused the wound on His body. The sage also fell on the ground with the impact of great love.

Therefore, you should have full trust in God. God doesn't just take care of his devotees; He takes care of everything. The whole insurance company is with Him. There are innumerable souls in this world. Some live on this earth, some fly in the sky, and some live in water. These creatures have no one who is responsible for them or protects them. They don't have any insurance companies. Still, they get everything they need to eat. Why should He not take care of you?

The Place of Anger

Q: What is the place of anger in an evolved person's life?

SM: An evolved person has very little anger left. His anger is like a child's. It stays with him only for a short time. It does not stay with him until he dies, like the anger of a snake or a camel.

The scriptures say that the best kind of person holds onto his anger only for a second, that an average person holds onto his anger for half an hour, and that an inferior person holds onto his anger for a day and a night. But a soul who is full of sins remembers his anger until he dies. When a person becomes angry, he should forget his anger quickly, because the longer he remembers it the more it will burn his heart. Anger, jealousy, and other emotions cause great restlessness inside.

Suppose that you decide to use a term of abuse against someone or to speak ill of someone. That person may or may not be affected, but you will be immediately affected, because the vibrations of your abusive words will be recorded on your internal tape. It is not good to become angry or emotionally upset. You should be aware that such emotions are your enemies. Lord Krishna says in the *Bhagavad Gita* that desire and anger arise from *rajoguna*, the force of passion, and that you should consider them your worst enemies. They will do you terrible harm. They work against your inner peace, bliss, and fulfillment. Krishna says, "O Arjuna, give up thinking of your external enemies. Instead, conquer your internal enemies."

Once a holy man was sitting on the bank of a river, repeating his mantra. On the same riverbank was a washerman. After the washerman had finished washing his clothes, he approached the holy man and said to him, "O Babaji, I want to go and have my food and also take a small nap. Please look after my donkeys for a while." The *sadhu* pretended not to hear. He just sat there repeating his mantra. After a couple of hours the washerman returned and saw that one of his donkeys was missing. He looked for the donkey but could not find it anywhere. The washerman was furious with the *sadhu*. He began to pull at his matted hair, shouting, "Where is my donkey?"

The *sadhu* replied, "What makes you think that I was sitting here to look after your donkey?"

The washerman said, "Even if you are a devotee of God, you could have done a little social work. You could have helped me."

The two began to argue with each other, and as the argument grew more heated both of them rolled up their sleeves and began to fight. The washerman was very healthy and strong because he got so much exercise washing clothes, but the *sadhu*, who never got any exercise, was frail and emaciated. Very easily, the washerman threw the *sadhu* to the ground and pummeled him. Just as the person who takes a beating gets tired, the person who gives it also gets tired. Soon both of them were sitting exhausted on the bank. After a couple of minutes, the *sadhu* got up and cleaned himself. He folded his hands and began to speak to God, saying, "O God, I have been praying to You for the past thirty years. For Your sake I have given up eating good food. I have lived in a forest and subsisted on roots. Nonetheless, when I was in trouble You did not come to help me."

Immediately a voice from heaven said, "O *sadhu*, I wanted to help you, but both of you were punching each other and I couldn't tell which was the washerman and which was the *sadhu!*"

This is the effect of anger. It completely changes your heart. Therefore, you should discard your tendency to become angry. If you control your anger, it turns into its opposite, love.

Once the great saint Rabi'a was asked, "Do you ever feel anger?"

"Yes," she replied, "but only when I forget God." If you fill your heart with devotion and love for God, there will be no room for anger.

I Didn't Tell You Not to Hiss

Q: When confronted with potential violence, should one take the position of self-defense or nonviolence?

SM: If you are completely stabilized in the state of nonviolence, then it is better to be in that state, but if you are not, then it is better to take the position of self-defense. These are times in which you have to defend yourself. There is no other way.

Once there was a big serpent who lived on the main street of a city. He used to bite many, many people. One day a saint came to live on the same street. The snake wanted to bite him too, but when he saw the saint he couldn't do it. This is the power of the state of nonviolence. When a person is established in that state, no one can be violent in his presence. The saint lived there for a while, and he instructed the snake until he was inspired to give up biting others. Then the saint blessed him and left.

The next year the saint came back again. This time he saw that the snake was in terrible shape. His bones were broken, his muscles were torn, and his tail was twisted. All the children in the neighborhood had been pulling his tail and throwing stones at him, so that by now the snake was half-dead. When the saint saw his condition, he asked, "O brother, why are you in such a predicament?"

"Should I speak the truth?" the snake asked. "This is the result of following your teaching. All the children of the town pull me and drag me by my tail and throw stones at me. I promised you that I would follow nonviolence, so I don't do anything."

"Now I'm going to give you further instructions," said the saint.

"Please," the snake replied, "they shouldn't make things any worse than they are now."

"No, no, this will be good," the saint said. "I told you not to bite, but I didn't tell you not to hiss. Whenever anyone walks by, just hiss at him as if you were about to bite. Then no one will come close to you."

The snake followed the saint's instructions. Whenever someone passed by, the snake would raise his head and make a hissing noise, and sure enough, no one would come close to him. The children stopped harassing him, and the snake regained his good health. It is important that we defend ourselves. If we always bear other people's violence, then these people will always be violent. If a violent person hits you and you hit him back, then you are actually being nonviolent, because you are stopping him from hitting many more people. Jesus said, "If somebody slaps your face, you should turn the other cheek." But sometimes a great being's teaching goes with a particular time and place. Our time is different. In our time turning the other cheek is like telling a person that he has done a good action, that it is okay to go around hitting people. So I say that if somebody hits you on your cheek, you should hit him on his cheek. If you do that, the person will stop harassing you.

The True Sign of Equal Vision Is Courage

A person should have great self-control and forbearance, but that does not mean that he should become so weak that if somebody attacks him, he says, "Great." When you have self-control, you conquer all your senses, and by conquering your senses, you gain great strength and energy.

In your heart and in your actions you should become humble. You should regard everyone as equal, for God dwells in everyone's heart. Shaivism says that the awareness of equality is the highest attainment. It is true religion. Everyone should have this attitude. You should look upon everything—plants, trees, religions, and other people—with equal vision. But that does not mean that you should become feeble. You should be very strong and courageous, and you should also have discrimination.

Swami Ramdas was a great yogi and the Guru of King Shivaji, a pious and righteous king. Ramdas had so much strength that he was able to do anything. He used to tell the stories of the *Ramayana* every day. One day while he was telling the stories, he began to explain, "Everything is Ram. The entire world is Ram." For a wise person this is true. If you lack understanding, then this is not true for you; still, it is true for me.

The next day, one of the king's elephants became crazy and began to run amuck. It started to run down the road, breaking this thing and that thing, snatching down this tree and that tree. It was causing a lot of trouble. When an elephant goes crazy like this, nobody can cool it down. You need the entire military.

Now Ramdas had a great disciple whose name was Kalyan Swami. As he was walking down the road, people began to stop him. They said, "O swami, don't go farther."

"Why?"

They said, "The king's elephant is running amuck. It might hurt you."

He said, "Don't you have any brains! Don't you know what my Baba said yesterday? He said, 'Ram is in everyone, in everything.' "

"It's very likely that Ram is in everything and everyone," the people said, "but please move aside."

Kalyan Swami said, "You have no understanding. *You* move aside."

He was a disciple of the great Samartha Ramdas. Who could say anything to him? So they all kept quiet. But even though the people understood that he was Ramdas's disciple, no animal was going to understand that. An animal never read the *Ramayana* in order to have that great understanding.

The elephant came towards him, and when it saw him it picked him up and squeezed him and threw him down onto the road. For Kalyan Swami, in the awareness of equality, only one moment was left.

At that point Samartha Ramdas and his entire group came running. Samartha Ramdas had great powers. He moved his hand over Kalyan Swami and brought him back to life. But after Kalyan revived, his pride came back to him. When a crazy person is fast asleep, he may not act crazy, but when he wakes up he becomes crazy once again.

Kalyan Swami said, "Didn't you tell me yesterday that Ram is in everyone and in everything? If that is true, how come that elephant attacked me?"

Ramdas asked, "Do you really remember that I said that?"

He said, "Absolutely. Because of that remembrance I walked in front of the elephant, and I was about to die."

Ramdas asked, "When you were walking down the road, three or four people stopped you and told you, 'Please do not go farther.' Wasn't Ram in them, too?"

It is great to practice the awareness of equality, but if such circumstances come up, you have to know what you are supposed to do. Having the awareness of equality does not mean that you should lack discrimination. Moreover, it does not mean that you should lack strength.

The scriptures speak at great length about the behavior that is appropriate at different times. There are scriptures in India that explain how to conduct oneself ethically while living in the world. For example, in the *Mahabharata* there is this question: "If a wicked person attacks me, how should I treat him, assuming I am a righteous person with an awareness of equality?" (In ancient India, a king had to learn all these things. To know how to govern a kingdom was part of spirituality.)

When you come in contact with someone, you should be able to see whether or not that person has the awareness of equality. You should understand whether he is a true human being or an elephant in the form of a human being. Even among human beings you find people who are like elephants, who are totally intoxicated with their own pride. If they are true human beings, then you can use your awareness of equality and explain to them the right way to behave, but if they are not this kind of person, you have to treat them differently.

Our scriptures say, "There are eight different kinds of human being. The eighth kind is a mere animal." In what way? The eighth kind of person will beat people. He will steal someone else's possessions. He will burn down buildings. He will shoot people for no good reason.

Now, according to the scriptures, if you come across the eighth kind of person and he tries to hit you, all that you can do is hit him back. Only then can you teach him a lesson. Such a person can learn only through blows. If you were to open the scriptures and try to give him the knowledge of the Truth, he wouldn't understand it. Therefore, the scriptures say that if you come across a person who is acting like an animal, then you have to respond to him accordingly. Only then will he become a true human being.

You must have heard about three holy places called Mathura, Gokul, and Vrindavan, where Shri Krishna lived and performed his sport. In Gokul there are more monkeys than there are people. When anybody passes by there, the monkeys jump down and take away that person's things and run away. So when people pass by, they carry a lot of fruit, and throw it to the monkeys so that they will leave them alone.

I didn't know this custom. Once I went on a pilgrimage to Gokul, and when I got there the monkeys began to nag me, too. There was no way out. I had only a blanket, which was around my body. I began to walk faster and almost broke into a run, and when I did that they began to follow me.

Now in India they use a stick as a weapon. I'm great at whirling a stick in the air. If I were to use a stick in that way, I could keep hundreds of people away from me. Even if you shot a bullet, it couldn't touch me. So as I began to run, the monkeys began to follow me. I had no food in my hand. I had no stick. I wondered what I should do. Just as the swamis wear a shawl around their shoulders, in the same way I had one. So I took the shawl, I tied a huge rock in the end of the shawl, and I began to twirl it. As I began to twirl it in the air, two or three monkeys were hit. They began to run away so fast, and I chased them.

There are human beings who are like these monkeys. When I was facing the monkeys, my *samatha*, my awareness of equality, had no effect on them. When they began to follow me, all that I could do was to take a huge rock and tie it in the end of my shawl, swirl it in the air, and hit their cheeks and make them run. I am against giving blows to animals; nevertheless, I am ready to teach them at any moment. It is very important to train them well. In the same way, when you are trying to teach a person something, you have to become his type. When you do that, you do not lose your awareness of equality. But you should not just live in the intoxication of spirituality. You should be practical, and you should know the discipline of the world and of the different actions of the world. You should always remember the strength and the power of the Self. You should always remember the teachings of your Guru.

In India there are many important swamis who are cowards.

They are cowards because they always want to maintain their pride
and honor. Many people go and sit before them and listen to their
lectures, and these swamis want to be sure that they do not look
foolish before their devotees. Now there are also some *sadhus* who
will go to a gathering like that and tell the swami, "I want to go on
a pilgrimage. Give me ten rupees." If the swami does not give him
the ten rupees immediately, the *sadhu* will begin to abuse him. He
will say, "What kind of swami are you? You have such a big ashram.
You have so many people. You are so prosperous. Why don't you
give me some money?" Then he will begin using abusive words.
When the *sadhu* speaks like that, the swami will become afraid and
will immediately put his hand in his pocket and give him ten rupees.

One of the *sadhus* who belonged to such a gang also came to
Muktananda Swami's ashram. He came up to him and said, "I want
fifty paise to smoke marijuana."

I said, "I'm not going to give you even one paise."

He said, "I'm going to get it from you."

I said, "You can take it when I give it to you! You had better
leave now."

Then he went down to the place where my Baba lived, and
came back to me the next day. He said, "I want some food."

I said, "Fine. During our mealtime come and eat."

"I want clothes."

"Fine. Take clothes." In the Ganeshpuri ashram we have these
things for *sadhus*. They can get their meals; they can get clothes.

He came back in the evening. He said, "Give me two rupees,
because I want to go to Kalyan."

I said, "I'm not a person who is going to give you money. A
sadhu does not need money. You can have clothes. You can have
meals, but not money. You don't have to go to Kalyan right away.
You don't have to file a case against anybody in court. It's not an
emergency case. You can walk there slowly. You can reach there in
eight days. I wandered around all of India on foot."

He said, "I'm going to get the money from you, you'll see."

Then he stood by the roadside, and abused me and abused me
and abused me. I had my lunch and went back to my room to take
a nap. At two-thirty I came out again. The *sadhu* was still by the
roadside, and he was still carrying on with his abusive terms.

I went out to the roadside and went closer to him. I spoke to him very gently, very softly and nicely. I told him, "Look, I'm not the kind of swami you think I am. I'm more wicked than you are. You should be really nice and just leave this place; just believe that I have surpassed you in wickedness. I have surpassed you." I said, "I'm whispering this to you because I know we are the same."

He said, "Nooo. I want to take the money from you."

I went inside. I had eaten a lot of abusive terms from him. Then I had my dinner and went to sleep.

The next day he was ready by the roadside to give me some more abusive terms. I said, "Now the time has arrived. I have to give him a lesson." I went before him and said, "Now, look. If your foolishness enters me, it's going to be terrible, but before that happens, you had better leave."

Now all the boys in the ashram began to tremble, wondering what the *sadhu* was going to do, because he had a long trident. He began to move his trident. So I got hold of the trident and gave him a blow. He fell on the ground, and I beat him.

I picked up his arm and lifted him up. I dragged him inside the ashram. He said, "Where are you taking me?"

I said, "Where do you think? We're going to dig up the earth and bury you alive!" Immediately he fell at my feet and said, "You are my father. Please, don't do this!"

I said, "Now you can go. Remember, you will find many more such swamis in the future."

So for that kind of person, that was the true awareness of equality. Because of my action, he dropped all the bad habits of his life. From that beating, he learned the wisdom of the highest Vedanta.

Of course you should have the awareness of equality. You should have love for others. You should have humility. You should also have courage and strength. If an animal comes before you, then you should know how to treat that animal. You should know how to make him become human. The true sign of equal awareness is courage.

The Nature of Dispassion

Q: What is dispassion, and what is its relationship to compassion?

SM: "Dispassion" is a word I use only in India. I never speak this word in the West. Lord Krishna describes the nature of the dispassionate person to his disciple Arjuna: "O Arjuna, he is dispassionate who has knowledge, who is alone all the time, whose mind is completely surrendered to Me." Such a person does not criticize others, nor does he listen to others' criticism. He is completely surrendered. He is without pretension. Some people have only a quarter in their pockets but they boast, "I have two hundred dollars in my pocket." This is not a sign of dispassion.

A dispassionate person is one who surrenders his mind completely to the Self. Such a person has gained control of his senses to such an extent that they function only with his permission. His senses have become indifferent to their objects. If the eyes continue to look for good things outside, the yogi tells them, "Stop looking at things outside; instead, turn inward and look at the Self." He controls his senses by continually turning them inward.

Tukaram Maharaj explains dispassion in a different way. He says, "He is a dispassionate being for whom all sense objects have become God. If such a person hears anything, he hears only God; if he sees anything, he sees only God. He is not interested in the doings of the marketplace; he is not interested in the comings and goings of daily life. He is completely absorbed in God, and God is his only object of thought, sight, hearing, and speech. He sees only God in front of him and behind him, above, below, and on all sides. This is the state of a truly dispassionate being."

Once there were a man and wife whose names were Ramka and Bamka. They were great devotees and had faith in the Self. One day they said to each other, "Let's give up our house and go to the holy city of Pandharpur. There we will be in the company of many *sadhus* and *mahatmas*, and we can live by begging alms." This is a recognized custom in India. On the way Bamka, the wife, had to go to the bathroom and stopped in a restroom by the side of the road. While Ramka was waiting for her, he caught sight of a big piece of gold lying in the road. He thought, "If my wife sees this, it may disturb her state of renunciation." So he began to cover the gold with dirt, looking from side to side, hoping to finish burying the gold before his wife returned. But Bamka had gone beyond her husband's state. She was a truly dispassionate being. When she returned, she saw what Ramka was doing. "Why are you covering dirt with dirt?" she asked. "Let's keep walking."

The *Bhagavad Gita* says that for one who has true dispassion all things—whether gold, stone, wood, or mud—are one and the same. True dispassion is remaining indifferent to duality, having love for nonduality, and having compassion for all beings. When the notion that other beings are different from oneself disappears, then compassion arises spontaneously from within.

Turn Your Attachments Toward God

Q: Should I try to give up my attachments forcefully or let meditation wash them away?

SM: You should expel them by meditation and right understanding. You should think about the nature of the things you are attached to. If you are attached to limited and perishable things, when they perish you will weep and lament. What is the use of an attachment that only brings you suffering? If you could turn your feeling of attachment toward the inner Self, toward God, then your attachment would be very good for you. Don't give up attachment; only turn it toward God and away from the things of this world.

Saint Tulsidas was very passionately attached to his wife. His wife was his five vital airs, his food, his drink, his father, his mother. She was east for him. She was west for him. She was every direction for him. He used to work as a priest, and sometimes while performing a ritual he would suddenly begin to miss his wife. He would leave the ceremony and rush home just to see her. Finally the wife got completely sick of all this; she decided to leave her husband and go to her parents' place. When Tulsidas returned one evening, he found the house empty; his wife had gone away, leaving him a note. Tulsidas was so upset that he could not eat or drink. He left for his in-laws' place immediately.

It was a dark and stormy night. Heavy rains were falling, and the river was in flood. The story writers say that it was so stormy and dark that one could hardly see one's way. Tulsidas crossed the river by riding on a corpse that he mistook for a log. He had become so blinded by his attachment to his wife that he could not distinguish one thing from another. The picture of his wife had taken seat in his eyes, and as a result he could see nothing but his wife.

When he reached the other shore, two fishermen were standing there. They were amazed to see that Tulsidas had crossed the river by riding on a corpse. These fishermen were from the same village as his wife, and they considered Tulsidas to be their own son-in-law, so they began to follow him. Now it happened that a python had come out into the storm. Pythons are not poisonous and do not bite, but they can swallow a person alive. If a python were to hold even an elephant in one of its coils, the elephant would not be able to get free. The python was lying on the road in front of the house of Tulsidas's in-laws. It was so huge that when it raised its head it was as high as the house. Mistaking the snake for a rope, Tulsidas climbed it to the first floor of the house, where his wife's room was. He knocked at the door, and she opened it.

When she came out, she was confronted by the vision of her husband. Down below, the two fishermen were knocking at the main door. They woke up the parents, who came out and asked, "What do you want?"

"We wonder what's happening with your son-in-law," said the fishermen. "We saw him riding a corpse!"

They went upstairs and asked Tulsidas, "How did you get up here?"

"I climbed a rope," he said. They lit a lamp and were terrified to see that the rope was really a python.

The wife was filled with remorse for having gone away. She said to herself, "He must be hopelessly attached to me if he was compelled to undertake a journey on such a dark and stormy night." She said to him, "You braved such a night; what was the reason?"

"It was for you," Tulsidas said.

His wife replied, "If you were as strongly attached to Lord Hari as you are to my body, which is mere dust, you would reach Vaikuntha without any difficulty. No one would be able to stop you."

Immediately these words sank into Tulsidas. At that moment he turned away from the house of his in-laws, away from the hopeless attachment to his wife, and became fully attached to God. The miracle of that new attachment was such that not only did he have a vision of Rama, but Rama became his constant companion. He would rub sandalwood on Rama, and Rama would apply the sacred mark on his forehead.

So provide a different object for your attachment and let that object be God. Become fully attached to Him. Then your attachment will bear great fruit for you.

When to Tell the Truth

Q: Is it always best to tell the truth? Sometimes it seems that telling the truth is impractical and not the right thing to do.

SM: It is right to speak the truth when it is appropriate. It is very good to be truthful. However, it is true that there are times when it is not useful, and at such times you should not reveal the truth. I will tell you a story that illustrates what I mean. There was a fakir who had a very good horse, which he used to ride every day. A caliph was living in the same town, and one day he saw the horse. He told the fakir, "This horse doesn't suit you. Sell it to me." The fakir replied, "I didn't become a fakir to earn money, and this horse is my best friend. I'm not going to sell it to you."

However, the caliph liked the horse so much that it became an obsession. It seemed that his whole life was focused on that horse. He plotted and plotted. One day he wrapped his leg in a piece of cloth and stationed himself on the street where the fakir used to ride. He began to moan, pretending that he was in great pain. When the fakir rode by, the caliph called, "O brother, please help me. It hurts, it hurts!"

"What's wrong with you?" the fakir asked.

"I fell on the ground and broke my leg," answered the caliph. "Please give me your horse so that I can ride home."

The fakir jumped off the horse and helped the caliph mount it. As soon as the caliph was seated, he gave the horse a big slap, and it began to run. As he rode off, the caliph shouted, "Damn you! Yesterday I asked you for the horse and you wouldn't give it to me. See whose horse this is now!"

The fakir yelled back, "Please, I'm offering my salutations to you; listen to my request. Take this horse and look after it, but don't tell anyone you stole it from me. If you tell others how you got this horse, they will learn how to cheat people; so please don't tell anyone how you got this horse."

The moment the caliph heard this, he turned around and rode back. He got down and gave the reins to the fakir. "Please forgive me," he said. "I made a great mistake. I coveted the property of a saint."

As the fakir said, sometimes you have to keep the truth secret, and sometimes it is best to reveal it.

The Meaning of Truth

Q: Do you know when people lie to you? How do you feel about it? Sometimes it seems more beneficial to tell a little falsehood than to hurt someone unnecessarily. Do you agree?

SM: If people tell a lie, certainly I will know it. Whether I know it or not, they will know it. There is somebody inside them who knows it.

The meaning of speaking the truth is very mysterious and profound. The truth should not become an obstacle or cause pain; it should not be bitter. You should not speak the truth in a way that will hurt people. If I spoke the bitter truth, then instead of making you laugh I would make you cry. The truth is like that sometimes.

Therefore, through understanding and contemplation, learn how to tell the truth. Do not ever lie. If a time comes when you cannot speak the truth, just observe silence. Then you will neither have to tell a lie nor have to tell the bitter truth. That is a great mantra.

See Only Good in Others

Q: Sometimes I meet people I don't especially like. What should I do about this?

SM: You should like yourself; whether or not you like other people is irrelevant. Constantly like yourself, and then feelings about other people will no longer trouble you. If you have to meet someone, you can do it very quickly. You don't have to imbibe his good or bad qualities. Even though another person may be bad, if you look upon him as good then your inner happiness will not change. Therefore, see only good things in others. No matter how bad someone may be, still there is something that exists in him which is very pure. Why don't you pay attention to the Self? Why do you concentrate on the actions that others perform?

Tulsidas used to say, "O Tulsi, in this world there are different kinds of people. You should learn how to mingle with all of them. Just as a boat on a river always floats in the direction of the current, you should accept whatever happens to you and whomever you meet without resistance."

You should not have the tendency to like one person and to dislike another. You should behave equally toward all. A great being said, "Don't consider anybody your enemy. Today's enemy can become tomorrow's friend, and today's friend can become tomorrow's enemy." For this reason the *Bhagavad Gita* says, "Have friendship toward all without any expectation." There is no one who deserves hatred.

The Sufi saint Lukman used to feed people with great respect every day. One day an old emaciated man turned up. All of the other people present prayed before they started to eat, but the old man remained silent. Lukman was annoyed. "Why are you not praying?" he asked. The old man replied, "I am not a worshipper of the pure Being. I am a worshipper of fire. As I am eating, I am worshipping fire." Lukman asked the old man to go away.

In the evening when he sat down to pray, Lukman heard a voice from the heavens say, "O Lukman, that old man was ninety years old. I have tolerated him for ninety years. The earth has tolerated him for ninety years. The air has tolerated him for ninety years. The water has tolerated him for ninety years. But you couldn't tolerate him even for a meal!" No matter who you are, you must never feel sick of people. You must be able to give them love.

6

God in the World

How to Attain God Without Leaving the World

When a person performs all his actions with supreme love and with the awareness that the Self is everywhere and in everything, his worldly life becomes spiritual. Then he does not have to follow any particular practice to find God. He does not have to give up his home and family. He does not have to go to an ashram or a temple. He can find God right where he is.

In one of Kabir's poems, God says, "O my dear one, where do you look for Me? I am with you." God is with all of us, but to understand this we have to understand the structure of the universe. This entire world came into manifestation because of the explosion of the bliss of God. It lives in God's bliss and finally merges into Him. All the forms in the universe are made of nothing but that bliss. The different activities of the world, its infinite and amazing modifications, its various names, its strange and diverse forms, its fascinating and remarkable arts, and its highly refined skills are all the joyful creation of the actor of the universe. Just as a spider spins a web out of its own body, God's Shakti, His own independent and inseparable power, created this universe out of its own being, manifesting it upon its own screen, in total freedom. It did not require any external material to create the universe because it had everything it needed within itself. That Shakti, that Consciousness, permeates every atom of this world. Vedanta says, *Brahmaiva sārvanāmāni rūpāni vividhāniccha* — "Brahman, the Absolute, is alone the substratum of all names, forms, and activities." All names and forms belong to Him. Whatever exists is God, and whatever does not exist is also God. For this reason, I say that there is nothing to give up which is different from you and nothing different from you to reject. There is no reason to look for Him from temple to temple, from church to church, because there is no place where He is not. A great being said, "What should I accept; what should I reject? Wherever I look, it is His own kingdom. He is the food, and it is He who offers food. He makes everyone become, and it is He who has become. Although He is one, He is many. When this is the case, what is the difference between being among people and being in a forest? What can you get from a religion, a yoga, or a *sadhana*? Doesn't He exist right within you? Is there anything except you? If there is something else, where is it?"

You may ask, "If God is everywhere, why then do we not experience Him?" You do not experience Him only because you do not really try to go within. You remain in the outside world, focusing your attention on external things. If you understood the outer world correctly, that would be fine. But instead, all that you see in it is duality and disparity.

You live only in the awareness of the different names and forms. You do not recognize the Truth that underlies them. You have your own delusion, your wrong understanding. It is an ancient delusion of the mind and society to which you have become accustomed. If you were to teach the future generation that gold is not gold, but iron, they would accept it. They would study it and learn about it and make everyone else believe it. Although unreal, the dealings of the marketplace go on with the guarantee of reality. In the same way, your delusion is sold with the guarantee of truth. However, in all religions it is He alone who exists. In all actions, in all castes, in all colors, it is He who exists, and they all belong to Him.

God and His Horse

When I was studying Vedanta, I heard a story about a rich shepherd named Ramja, who worshipped a form of God called Khandoba. (In India people worship God in many different forms, even though their underlying understanding is that God is attributeless. We who are Consciousness have become matter just to perform actions. When we can become this, why cannot God, who is Consciousness, also take a form?) This shepherd had a golden statue of Khandoba and also one of his horse.

One day all of Ramja's sheep died, and he became poverty-stricken. Someone gave him a suggestion: "Your statue of God is made of gold. Why don't you sell the statue and buy sheep and when you become rich once again have another statue made?"

When a person is in difficult circumstances, he will do anything. Ramja took his statue to a jeweler and asked, "What will you pay me for my deity and his horse?"

The jeweler weighed both objects. The image of God weighed one kilo, and his horse weighed two kilos. The jeweler said, "Your God weighs one kilo, so I will pay you one hundred thousand rupees for it. The horse weighs two kilos, so I will pay you two hundred thousand rupees for that."

The shepherd was furious. "You value my God at only one hundred thousand rupees and his horse at two hundred thousand?" he cried. "Have you no brains?"

The jeweler explained, "Brother, for you there is God and his horse. For me there is only gold."

You are just like the shepherd. You do not realize that the Lord of the world exists in the form of this world.

A great being wrote:

> No matter how many ornaments you make from gold,
>   they are all gold.
> Gold is within the ornaments,
>   and the ornaments are within the gold.
> There is gold inside and gold outside, and all
>   these forms are created from the one gold.

Yari Sahib was a great Sufi being who said, "Understand gold and remove all your concepts about the ornaments. If you have this awareness, then what is high and what is low?" The universe is infinite, but although the Self of the universe has become many, it remains one.

The Play of the Lord

When you awaken your own inner Consciousness from within, you realize that just as different bulbs are illuminated by the same electrical power, the light of Shiva is in all the objects of creation. It is said that in the beginning God was alone. But then He had a thought: "Let Me become many." Because God could not act out His drama by Himself, for His own pleasure He became many, assuming all the strange and unique forms in the universe. This creation is God's ceaseless play, His unique drama, which He performs for His own amusement. It is an enchanting piece of magic, but it is real. All of us are players on His great stage, which is this world. One of the aphorisms in the *Shiva Sutras* is, "The Self is the actor." It means that the supreme Truth changes its true nature and wears different costumes. Assuming different roles, such as the waking, dream, and deep sleep states, it plays in the world. Kashmir Shaivism says:

> O God, You are always intent on playing this game.
> You take delight in creating and maintaining this world.
> You find satisfaction in reabsorbing it into Yourself.
> You take away our pain and our suffering.

Shaivism says that God has two aspects. He is both transcendent and immanent. In His transcendental aspect He is supremely pure and beyond this world, but in His immanent aspect He is within the world. True humanity is to see God's divine and unchanging face in His constantly changing drama. This is the correct understanding, which arose from the contemplation of the great sages who had transcended their minds. The inner knowledge manifests in the outer world. The outflowing of the joy of the inner Consciousness manifests as the magnificence of the outer world.

It is true that there are infinite modifications in this world—birth and death, pain and pleasure, health and sickness. Some people cry and others laugh. But that is the nature of the drama. When I was very young, I saw a play in which a thief killed two people. I cried bitterly, but the people sitting next to me reassured me by saying, "Don't worry; it's only a play." This is what the world is. It is a play of the Lord. The only reason we experience pain in this world is because we have not recognized the nature of this play.

In the *Yoga Vasishtha* the sage Vasishtha told Lord Rama, "The world is as you see it." Creation is not different from your outlook. In whatever way you understand this universe of Consciousness, that is what it becomes for you. If you see it as favorable, it is favorable. If you see it as unfavorable, it is unfavorable.

Once there was a fair. A great being who was established in the state of steady wisdom wanted to go there. On his way to the fair he was passing through a forest. He found a huge tree and sat down beneath it. The shade was beautiful and cool, and as he sat there he entered the state of meditation. He became totally absorbed in himself and God.

As he was sitting there, two addicts approached, smoking marijuana. It was very hot, and they were totally high. They needed the help of the shade. As they sat down, they noticed the fakir sitting under the same tree, and they said to each other, "He smoked more than we did. At least we are conscious!"

Then a person who drank vodka approached, a half-empty bottle in his pocket. He too was getting very hot, so he sat under the same tree. He was not totally intoxicated, so he was not yet seeing double. He could see one person as one person. The drunkard said, "Look at their predicament. Maybe they drank just a bit, but they're totally intoxicated. I drank half a bottle, but I'm still okay."

They were all under the tree, and everyone was taking rest in his own way, to make himself comfortable. A fourth person approached. He was a thief. All night he had put forth a lot of self-effort, but he had only been able to steal a few things. He was exhausted and also wanted to take rest. Fatigue follows everyone. Even after you dance or watch a movie you feel exhausted. Fatigue and external happiness are one.

The thief saw everyone else lying on the ground. He said to himself, "Look at these thieves. They must have been stealing all night, but they haven't gained anything. They look so exhausted. Although I worked so hard last night, I still feel fine."

A fifth person approached. He was a sadhu, and he was very intelligent and had a lot of understanding. When he saw the great being, he became very happy. He said, "What a great being! He's so absorbed." He sat down before him and became totally immersed in ecstasy.

However, the thief wanted to do his next job. He went to the intelligent sadhu and asked him, "Why are you sitting here? Everybody's unconscious. Let's go on to the other town."

The intelligent sadhu replied, "This one is a great being. Let us sit here."

The thief said, "You have lost your understanding. He must have stolen something at the other place. That's why he's just lying there."

The drunkard looked up and said, "What kind of understanding do you have? He must be drunk; that's why he's unconscious."

The marijuana addict said, "He has smoked a lot of marijuana, and because it was so hot he became unconscious."

This is how people project their own outlook onto the creation. It is because you see everything through the glasses of your own outlook that you see so many differences and disparities in this world. Otherwise, this world is nothing but the Lord of the world. Everyone is an image of God. Everyone is the form of the supreme Truth. In the *Bhagavad Gita* the Lord says, "O Arjuna, I am the same to all beings. None is hateful or dear to Me." No matter who goes to the ocean to swim, the coolness of the water is the same. Similarly, there is no flaw in any object in this world; the only flaw is in your own vision. There is no duality in this world; the only duality is in your attitude. When you turn within and see the Self, you will understand that everything has sprung from the Truth and that therefore everything is the Truth. Then you will understand that you do not have to give up your children, because they will not interfere with your attaining God. You do not have to hate society, because in society, too, it is He alone who exists. You do not have to give up your household activities, retreat to a forest, and meditate with your eyes closed. All that you have to do is understand that it is He alone who exists in all your activities and that all the actions you perform are His worship. If you have this awareness, how can God be far from you? If you have this awareness, then your life itself becomes yoga, meditation, and knowledge. If you have this awareness, all knowledge arises from within and you become the embodiment of God.

The Flowers of Your Actions

In the eighteenth chapter of the *Bhagavad Gita*, Lord Krishna gives the conclusion of His teachings to Arjuna: "By worshipping Him from whom all beings have evolved and by whom all this is pervaded, through the performance of one's duty, one attains perfection." Commenting on this verse, Jnaneshwar Maharaj wrote, "O Arjuna, consider all your actions as flowers to be offered to Him in whom this entire world exists. When you worship Him with the flowers of your actions, God's joy is boundless."

A husband should be a true husband to his wife, and a wife should be a true wife to her husband. A mother should be a true mother to her children, and the children should be true children to their mother. There should be love between them, and they should offer the flowers of their feelings and actions to God. If you worship God in this way, you will experience limitless joy. But if you do not worship God in the right way, how can you experience any joy in the world?

Many great beings were householders. One of them was Tukaram Maharaj. He worked in the fields, considering both the fields and his work to be God. Namdev was a tailor who attained God while sewing clothes. It is said that although God is formless and attributeless, still He assumed a form for Namdev's sake. Sautamali was a gardener who found God while working in his garden. He used to grow eggplant, and he would say, "My Lord dwells in the eggplant." Janabai was a maid who attained God while grinding wheat. Sometimes when she was exhausted from working, God would take a form and grind with her. Ramdas was a cobbler and attained God while mending shoes. Kanupatra was a dancer and a prostitute, and she attained God while doing that work. Mirabai was a queen. Rabi'a Basri was such a great saint that if she did not visit the sacred stone of Mecca, it would come to her. She was sold as a slave to a rich merchant and realized the Self during her period of slavery. Nauroji was a thief who went to rob the great being Chaitanya Mahaprabhu, but the great being robbed the thief, and Nauroji became a great devotee. Among the Sufis there was a robber chief named Fazil-aza, who later became a saint. Do not think that you should start robbing banks. I am telling you this only to explain that you can attain God in your own field of action.

When you perceive the Lord of all everywhere and worship Him through your own actions, you attain great worthiness. Jnaneshwar Maharaj said that if, while performing your duty and staying with your family, you perceive Him in your heart, you will experience the highest knowledge. Spontaneously, through meditation, you will attain the state of absorption.

There is no word or object or place or time where Consciousness is not. Shaivism says, "The experiencer himself continues to exist always and everywhere as the object of experience." God is the experiencer as well as the experienced. God understands everything through your feelings. Not only does He understand everything, but because He exists in each object in the form of knowledge, you are able to know objects. It is God who, in the form of knowledge, is known through every object. God is both *prakasha* and *vimarsha*. As *prakasha*, He illumines everything in this world. As *vimarsha*, He is known through every object. Just as God is in everything, He is also in you. A word contains its own meaning and is inseparable from it. In the same way, God exists in every human being in the form of Consciousness. There is no state without Him.

In the *Bhagavad Gita* the Lord says that it is the inner Self which functions through all the senses. It is That which sees, smells, hears, and tastes. It is That which comes and goes, which sleeps and awakens, which inhales and exhales. Everything is the work of the Self, of Consciousness. Once you know your own Self through understanding and meditation, you will know that you cannot be different from bliss. Shaivism says, "You have lost your own Self within yourself. Therefore, find it there. Make your own Self manifest within you."

Constantly meditate on your own Self. Don't try to renounce one thing and embrace something else. Give up all these involvements. Once you know your Self, you will develop great interest in leading your life. And you will lead a great life, because if you know your Self, you will know others. Now you may find your wife very sour and bitter, but once you know your Self the same wife will be as sweet to you as nectar. Now you may find your husband to be a torturer, but once you know your Self the same husband will seem delicious.

You Alone Exist

A great sage in Shaivism said, "Do your *sadhana* with the awareness, 'I am Shiva and everything else is Shiva.'" Even if you perceive differences, even if you see duality, maintain this awareness for your *sadhana*. Shiva is the enjoyer as well as all objects of enjoyment. The seer is Shiva, and the seen is Shiva. Shiva is the husband, and Shiva is the wife. Shiva is the one who performs an action, Shiva is the instruments of action, and Shiva is the action itself. With this awareness of Shiva, do the *sadhana* of Shiva. Only God exists in this world. Therefore, do not give up your family life, do not leave your children, do not spoil your relationship with your husband or wife, do not see faults in your society, and do not beat your head, worrying about the times and death. This world is the strange play of the Lord of all plays, and you have a very small role in His drama. Play it very well, so that everyone can say, "Encore, encore!"

The Nectar of This World

A great being said, "This world is the beautiful garden of Shiva, of the Lord, made so that you can walk in it with great joy." The world does not exist so that you can have attachment, aversion, jealousy, envy, or hatred. It does not exist for you to fight with other people and die. Do not burn in the fire of desires, wanting this and wanting that. Simply accept whatever comes to you through God's grace. Do not worry about anything and be ecstatic in the garden of Shiva. When people come, let them come; when they go, let them go. This world is an image created by Shiva. Due to your lack of understanding you do not know this, and because of that you betray yourself. Because you do not recognize that Shiva permeates this entire world, you see the world as something else and, for no good reason, you fear.

Once three great beings, Lord Buddha, Confucius, and Lao-tse, got together in heaven to discuss the nature of the world. In the middle of their discussion, a heavenly nymph appeared before them holding a golden cup. "Take this cup," she said. "It contains the elixir of the world. If you taste it, you will know the real nature of this world."

First, Buddha took the cup. As soon as he tasted the elixir he spat it out, saying, "Ugh, this is poisonous. You cannot find anything worse than this. It is disgusting." Of course, he concluded that the world was terrible. He had left his wife and child when he was very young. How could he say that the world was sweet?

Then the nymph told Lao-tse, "You taste it."

Lao-tse took a sip and said, "It's all right. It's neither bitter nor sweet."

Finally, the nymph gave the cup to Confucius. He took one sip and then another. He drank and drank, until he had emptied the cup. He said, "Whether this world is bitter or sweet depends on how you taste it. If you drink the elixir of this world with love for God, then it becomes nectar for you."

If you remember the Self all the time, you will find delight in this world.

Peace in the World

Q: In the ashram I experience a lot of peace. What should I do to attain the same peace even in the world?

SM: Make the peace become completely established in your heart and take it back to the world. Then, no matter where you go, you will experience the same peace. Once peace becomes firmly established in your heart, you will not experience any anxiety. You will experience only peace.

People who lacked understanding hanged the great Sufi saint Mansur Mastana. He had not done anything wrong. He had not stolen anything. He had not committed any sins, nor had he plotted anything. All he had done was speak the truth. He said that this whole world is an illusion and that only the Truth exists. Because he said this, he was hanged. He had lost himself completely in the Truth, so much so that he did not even know where his body was. They accused Mansur Mastana because he said, "Anal-haq, I am God, I am the Truth." Even when he was being hanged, all that he said was, "Anal-haq." His awareness, "I am God," never changed, not even when he was being hanged. He never experienced anxiety.

It is very good that you are experiencing peace here. Once that peace becomes completely established in your own heart, it can never be destroyed. That peace is indestructible. In *Jnaneshwari*, Jnaneshwar Maharaj said that the Lord gave the experience of *samadhi* to Arjuna; afterward, He did not send him to a cave or to a mountain resort or to a bungalow. He made him fight in the battlefield, which means that He made him do his own work and put forth his own effort.

The peace that you have attained will remain when you are engaged in your daily duties; it will never be obstructed. Once you experience peace it never leaves you. It becomes completely established in you; it takes residence in you. Truly speaking, a person experiences fun in life only after he attains peace. Without peace, the world is not a world. It is a cemetery; it is a graveyard of weeping. Eknath Maharaj was a great saint from Maharashtra. He said, "I will lead my life in this world with great joy, with great happiness, and with great love and bliss."

My Babaji used to meet at least five thousand people every day. He used to listen to everyone's weeping and wailing. Babaji never got angry with anyone, nor did he ever get fed up with anyone. People belonged to him. How could he get fed up with them? I am the same way. Some people gave me a suggestion, saying, "Your health is not that good; you should go somewhere else for a rest." I said, "I'm the head of such a big family. How can I give up my big family and go somewhere else?"

Shaivism teaches that the joy you feel among people, the joy you feel in community, is the experience of *samadhi.* So why sit in a cave like a mouse with your eyes closed? If you experience peace in the ashram, then consider the whole earth the ashram; then you will experience unobstructed peace everywhere. Do not consider the ashram only a few acres of land. Consider all directions, from east to west, from north to south, the ashram.

I read the poem of a great being, who said, "When the whole forest becomes the sacred plant *tulsi,* when all the stones become the sacred stone Shaligram, when all rivers become the holy Ganga, at that moment Rama will reveal Himself within you." This is truly how it is.

Spiritual Marriage

Q: Please describe the roles of the husband and wife in an ideal spiritual marriage.

SM: A husband and wife have great responsibility toward each other.
They should see each other as divine. The husband should be God
for the wife, and the wife should be God for the husband. If they
can see each other in this way, it will be good for both of them.
The husband and the wife should live together not just to satisfy
their sensual desires, but to satisfy the inner Self through meditation.
Both of them should be aware of God in all their activities, as they
attend to every single part of their daily schedule. They should be
absorbed in each other, they should love each other, but that does
not mean that they should always be rubbing their bodies together.
That kind of love doesn't mean anything.

The Sanskrit word for wedding is *panigrahana*, which means
"hold each other's hand." Once a man and a woman put their hands
together, they must make sure they never separate. A husband and
wife should develop trust for each other; they should maintain that
trust and live with it. If they do not surrender to each other, if
there is mistrust between them, then they will be married in the
morning and divorced in the evening. If they hold themselves back
from each other, if they do not give themselves to each other
completely, the marriage breaks up. If they give their hearts to each
other, there is no way they can take them back; there is no way
they can take their love back. If they do, their marriage is not a real
marriage.

A true incident took place in India. The mother of the world,
Parvati, was observing severe *tapasya*, severe austerities, because
she wanted to marry Lord Shankar. Now Shankaraji's abode was a
graveyard, and his appearance was shocking. He wore tattered tiger
skins, and he applied the ashes of dead bodies all over his body.
He lived in this graveyard in great ecstasy.

Parvati was a princess, the daughter of a great king. Nonetheless,
she was determined to marry Shankar. There was another deity
called Vishnu, who was also great in his own way. He adorned
himself very beautifully with ornments on his head and covering
his entire body. His abode, Vaikuntha, was great. Parvati's father
said to her, "You should marry Vishnu. Why do you want to marry
Shankar, who lives in a cemetery?"

Vishnu sent Narada, a swami, to reason with Parvati, but she
replied, "O swami, go and give the knowledge of yoga to others;
give the knowledge of the Truth to others, not to me. You don't
know anything about this! I gave my heart, I gave my love to Shankar.

There is no way I can take it back from him. I have already given myself to him."

If you offer your heart to someone and then take it back, you are a cheat. You are merely deceiving that person, and there is no truth in your action. Therefore, a husband and wife should become absorbed in each other.

An ideal spiritual union is that in which the husband and wife have become so absorbed in each other that when the husband eats, the wife is satisfied, and when the wife eats, the husband is satisfied. The *dharma*, the duty, of marriage is that the husband and wife live together as though they were one. If they remain two, there is no point to the marriage. Only the words "husband" and "wife" should be different. The two people should be one. The wife should become the husband's soul, and the husband should become the wife's soul. They should each live for the benefit of the other and not live selfishly. They should be caught in the embrace of pure love, and they should never be able to get out of that embrace. This is an ideal spiritual marriage.

In such a marriage the husband and the wife remain immersed in God all the time. If their awareness is continually in God, if they live without either attachment or animosity, their life together will be the playground of God. The child that comes from such a union will grow into a very great being and do tremendous work in the world. This is the kind of marriage the scriptures recommend. If you lead your household life with great understanding and according to the scriptures, there will be great joy in it.

The purpose of leading a family life is to learn to love the members of your family more and more. If you cannot love your family, how can you love God? You experience love first of all for other people; only later do you turn it toward God. However, we use this kind of life to learn how to hate each other. If a husband and wife have no self-control and no love for God, then both of them will beat their heads and constantly weep. But if they live together with great respect, worshipping God, there will be no weeping in their family.

Change Your Understanding

Q: I don't think my family life is going well; my wife and I are always bickering. Should we separate?

SM: No, no, no! If you separate, you will want to remarry, and once again you will have the same problems. All wives and all husbands are the same, so don't change your husband or your wife. Change your nature. Then everything will be all right.

A husband and wife should live together as friends. A husband should look upon his wife as God, and a wife should look upon her husband as God. Only then will family life be filled with joy. The Upanishads say, "It is God who takes the form of a man and becomes a husband. It is God who takes the form of a woman and becomes a wife." If a husband and wife do not have this understanding, they will always be like two pots floating on water, clashing against each other with every wave.

So change your understanding. Don't destroy your family life and home because of your petty conversations and quarrels. Instead, have self-control and discrimination. Forget the past; lead your life in this way, and within a moment everything will change.

Once Sheikh Nasrudin and his wife Fatima were quarreling about who should take the donkey to graze. Nasrudin said, "Every day I take the donkey out. Today you should take it out."

"Absolutely not!" said Fatima. "Every day I cook, so why shouldn't you take the donkey out?"

The quarrel became more and more intense, and they began to fight. Finally, they came to an agreement. Nasrudin said, "Look, Fatima, there is no fun in fighting like this. We should observe silence. Whoever breaks the silence will have to take the donkey out."

Realizing that if she remained with her husband she might speak first, Fatima went to a neighbor's house. Days passed. The donkey was starving. Nasrudin had no one to cook for him, so he too was hungry. His son was hungry. The neighbors were very poor, so even Fatima was hungry. All the townspeople knew that Nasrudin had taken a vow of silence, so some thieves decided to break into his house. They stole everything—even the turban from Nasrudin's head—but he did not say so much as a word.

In the meantime Fatima's son was visiting her. She was feeling a little compassion, so she prepared some soup, gave some of it to her son, and told him in sign language to take the rest of it to Nasrudin. The boy took the soup to the house and saw that it had been ransacked. Nothing was left.

"O father," he said, "what were you doing when the thieves stole everything?" Nasrudin made no reply. Then the son offered his father some soup. "Take it," he said. Nasrudin still did not want to speak, so he began to gesture. He tried to explain how his turban had been stolen by pointing at his head. The boy thought that the father was showing him where to pour the soup, so he emptied the bowl of hot soup right on Nasrudin's head. Without waiting for his father's reaction, he ran to his mother to give her the news.

"O mother," he cried. "Everything was taken from the house; everything was stolen." Fatima ran home and saw that everything she owned was gone. Then she saw Nasrudin sitting quietly in a corner. She screamed at him, "What kind of scoundrel are you? Couldn't you see what the thieves were doing? Why didn't you stop them?"

Nasrudin said, "You spoke first. Take the donkey out."

Do not be like Nasrudin. Do not let your home be destroyed for the sake of a petty quarrel. A husband and wife should have some discrimination and should live together with great joy.

In the Mold of Their Parents' Feelings

Q: What is the best way to raise our children?

SM: You should consider your children divine beings and transmit good vibrations to them. You should give them good training and help them develop good habits. You should also treat them with great respect, so that they can imbibe that respect into their lives. The more love and respect parents give to their children, the more sublime and great the children will be.

All the saints have said that parents, especially mothers, can train their children in whatever way they want. However, before thinking about how to raise their children, parents should first make themselves very good. Children come out of the parents' own bodies; they are created from the parents' blood and sexual fluid. You all know about hereditary diseases. If your grandfather or even your great-grandfather had a disease like diabetes or high blood pressure, you can also get that disease, because these diseases are contained in the essential fluids of their bodies and are passed down through the sexual fluid. In the same way, parents' feelings come down to their children. If a husband and wife perform good actions and have good feelings, then the children born to them will be the same. Children are made in the mold of their parents' feelings; whatever the parents are is what the children become. Therefore a father and mother should behave very well. They should become very virtuous. Goodness should permeate their bodies. Then they will not have any problems with their children.

In India there was a king who was deeply religious. He had lived according to the highest principles; he had faith in God and he was very pure. However, he was blessed with a son who, when he grew up, began to act in a very strange way: he started plundering not only the people, but even the royal treasury. The people could not understand this, so one day a delegation went to the king and asked him, "O Your Majesty, you are such a noble being. How could you have produced such a bandit?"

The king replied, "I do not blame him. He was created from my own sexual fluid."

"But if he has your blood in him, he cannot be a bandit."

The king then told this story. "There was a time when I was constantly at war. I was engaged in invading smaller kingdoms. My mind was constantly thinking of conquering other countries. It was at that time that I conceived the child. The state of my mind permeated my sexual fluid, and the child imbibed these feelings into the essence of his own being. That is why he grew up to be a bandit."

This is why, when people ask me how they can improve their children, I always tell them to improve themselves first. If parents become very disciplined, very pure, and very strong, they will see what kind of fruit they will obtain from the seed they sow.

People make children without understanding the true secret of creating a good child. Today many children are mentally sick. Why is this so? It is because of defects in the actions, feelings, and hearts of their parents. I have met every sort of person in this world. I have met the worst person and the best person in this world, and I am the Guru of all types of people. Whoever meets me tells me his life story. I am a good listener; I never get tired of listening to people. So I know how these things happen. First of all, when the parents get together, they do not really get together with love. They are not completely together. Also, they smoke marijuana or drink alcohol. They take these things in large quantities, and then they try to make children. These heavy intoxicants affect the elements of the body. When something goes wrong with the elements of the body, the sexual fluid becomes agitated. When children are conceived under these conditions, they suffer mentally.

Our scriptures explain that when two people get together to make a child, they should be in a very beautiful place, and they should have great love for each other. They should eat rich food. They should have high thoughts. These are the conditions under which a good child can be produced. Whatever qualities the parents have will automatically be imbibed by the child.

In ancient times there was a queen named Madalasa. Madalasa's father was a perfect being, a great sage. He taught yoga and wisdom to his daughter and made her complete. She married a prince, who later became the king, and she began to have children.

Every pore of Madalasa's body was filled with the awareness of the Absolute. The great being Tukaram said, "Through meditation, knowledge, and chanting, not only the Self but the entire body becomes the Absolute." The *Vijnana Bhairava* says that once you know the supreme Principle, not only does your Self become the supreme Principle, but your entire body from head to toe becomes the embodiment of Consciousness.

Whenever Madalasa conceived a child, she would think about the Self. While she carried the child in her womb, she would fill herself with the awareness of Brahman, the Absolute. After the child was born, she would put him in a cradle, and as she rocked him she would sing, "O my child, you are ancient; you are the Truth; you are Consciousness; you are the supreme Brahman; you are the Absolute." Her lullabies were very beautiful; great beings still sing them.

Madalasa had seven sons. Because all of them were conceived and cared for in this way, when they grew up they became yogis, attained the state of Parabrahman, and left home. After they had all gone, the king said to Madalasa, "What have you done? Someone has to succeed to the throne. After all, I am a king, and when I am gone someone has to take care of the kingdom!"

"Don't worry," Madalasa said. "One more child will be born."

When the eighth child was born, Madalasa began to teach him

differently. She sang, "You are very brave; you are very courageous. You will take care of your subjects with great righteousness." When that child grew up, he sat on the throne.

Whatever parents want their children to learn, they should first learn themselves. They should imbibe it into the essence of their own systems. They should make it alive in the atmosphere of their own home. Then they won't have to teach their children anything. Their own state will affect their children very naturally. If they think highly of themselves, if they remember again and again that the same supreme Truth lives within them, if they live in a state of continual remembrance of that Truth, then their children will naturally grow into beautiful beings.

Disciplining Children

Q: Discipline and control are two general concerns that parents have. How can parents know how much discipline to use?

SM: Parents do not have to be concerned about disciplining and controlling their children. Parents should first see whether they themselves are following discipline. If they are, then their children will be disciplined too. For example, I am the head of an ashram. If I do not follow the ashram discipline, how can I expect others to follow it? Will the discipline fall from the sky? Just as people in the ashram learn by example, children take on their parents' qualities through their example. If the parents are disciplined, have love and respect for each other, and take interest in each other, their children will naturally imbibe these qualities.

When I was still very young, I was living in the town of Yeola. There was a pious man called Sitaram Jacoosa, a weaver of silk cloth, who used to invite me to his house for lunch once a week. One day we were talking together before lunch. He had just lit a cigarette and was about to smoke it when his son came in to call us for lunch. I did not see the son coming, but all of a sudden I saw Jacoosa extinguish the cigarette and put it under his mat. Then he rubbed his face and sat there as though he weren't doing anything. He looked so scared that I thought perhaps some great man had come. Then I looked up and saw that his young son was standing there.

After we finished our lunch, Jacoosa walked with me to the place where I stayed. While we were walking I asked him, "Why did you suddenly put out your cigarette and clean your face? What were you afraid of?"

"I did it because my young son came into the room," he said.

"You are so afraid of your own child?" I asked.

"No, it is not that I am afraid of my son. I am afraid that if my son saw me smoking he would say, 'It's all right for me to smoke because my dad is smoking.'"

When I heard that I realized that it was a good lesson—not that parents should do things behind their children's backs, but that they should set an example for their children.

When parents are with their children, they should behave in such a way that the children won't imbibe any bad qualities but will learn only good ones. It is better if parents don't fight, but if they are addicted to fighting they should do it in the privacy of their bedroom, where the children cannot see or hear. Sometimes a parent complains to me, "My son swears." When I ask the child where he learned this, he says, "My parents fight a lot and they use these words; I learned to swear from them."

Instead of complaining, parents should lead a good and beautiful life for the sake of their children. They should set an example for their children through consistently good behavior, love, and peacefulness and by maintaining a close relationship with them.

Forgiving Your Parents

Q: I have a great deal of anger and resentment against my mother. This seems to be the obstacle that prevents me from experiencing love. I ask for your help.

SM: Give up your anger and resentment. Whoever she is, she is your mother. For this reason, you should not be ungrateful to her. Maybe you hate her because she does not act according to your interest. However, she held you inside her womb for nine months. Even after that, she took very good care of you at least for a few years. So she has been good to you.

Even if a father, a mother, a Guru, or a friend has done cruel things to you, the greatest humanity is to forgive them. If you continue to remember these things, they will hurt you from within. Maybe your mother has behaved badly toward you. However, her bad behavior belongs to her. You should forget it. I read a story about a great being who, just before he left his body, gave a final teaching to his disciples. He said, "Do four things. First of all, do not ever remember that you helped a person. Second, if anybody has wronged you, forgive him; never take revenge. Third, death is always behind you; therefore, find some means to overcome it. Finally, make your house the house of God." Do not have resentment and hatred in your heart toward anyone. Forget what your mother has done to you. Have only good thoughts. If you want to uplift yourself, you should maintain good understanding at all times. Taking revenge or remembering others' mistakes is not the sign of a wise person.

A Simple Life

Q: Is it better for the spirit to be involved in simple life work, such as raising children and housework, or in developing a professional career?

SM: First you yourself should become simple. Then the whole world and everything in it will become very simple, too. Everything will come under the category of a simple life.

Selfless Work

Q: How should I approach my work?

SM: You should become completely immersed in your work. First, however, you should examine your motives and your attitudes. You should decide what your purpose is in doing the kind of work you do. Reflecting on these questions leads to more basic questions: Who am I? What is the purpose of my existence? What is my relationship with the Creator? This inquiry will lead to the discovery that you belong to the Creator and that you should work entirely for His satisfaction. People work because it is His law that everyone should work. Work should be offered as a ritual sacrifice to Him and Him alone. It should be done with reverence.

If you work from a selfish motive, you become liable to self-deception. Work must be done without selfish motive whether it is worldly work or spiritual work. In fact, there is no difference between the worldly and the spiritual, and this becomes clear when you gain right understanding. Before that, the worldly and spiritual appear to be antagonistic. The world, which appears to be so diverse, which you perceive sometimes as favorable and sometimes as unfavorable, sometimes as full of agreeable things and sometimes disagreeable things, is really nothing but the expansion of the one Lord. The world is not an illusion; it is not *maya* nor is it a brief episode. The world is as real as God. This is the true knowledge of the nature of the world.

In the *Bhagavad Gita*, Lord Krishna says that the same supreme Being stretches in all directions. All activities and pursuits, all names and forms, are only different manifestations of the Truth. Because this is the case, there is no work which is an obstacle on the spiritual path. Anyone who worships God while following his vocation is fulfilling the purpose of his birth. For example, a musician can worship God with music, provided that he has no selfish motive. A teacher can worship God by teaching, provided that he teaches selflessly. A businessman can worship God in his business, provided that he does it without selfish motive. A farmer can worship God by raising crops, provided that he does it selflessly. Doing one's work selflessly means dedicating it to God. No matter what your pursuit in the world, if you dedicate it to God it becomes a spiritual pursuit. If you are full of this awareness toward your work, you will always be able to do it in the right manner, understanding that all work is a way of serving the Lord, that it is nothing but a divine *yajna*, a divine sacrifice, and you will always be free of selfish motives.

You should perform your work, your service in the world, as selflessly as the elements perform their services to us. Take the case of water. We wash our bodies with water, we drink it, and we use it in so many other ways. Water has never complained. Water has allowed itself to be used by us without expecting anything from us, without making any demands on us. Take the case of air. Our lives depend on it; we are constantly taking in air with our lungs. Yet air does not ask anything from us; it serves us in the most selfless manner. Take the case of fire and of earth; they sustain us all with no selfish motive. The same is true of space. When air, earth, fire, water, and space do not expect anything from us, when they do not make any demands on us, why should we have any selfish desires? Why can we not work as selflessly as the elements?

The essential message of the *Gita* is that we have the right to perform an action but not to reap its fruits. So while doing your work, you should not seek any reward for yourself; do not seek any fruits for yourself. While doing your work, become completely one with it. Work is its own reward. Doing work skillfully is an end in itself. You should do your work with skill, with intelligence, with understanding, and with efficiency, but without expecting any reward, without seeking any selfish gratification.

The Lords' Club

Q: Why do we feel the need to do some special job or be someone special in order to feel complete, instead of just being ourselves? How can we remain detached even if we don't hold a high position?

SM: The desire for a high position is your downfall. If you don't have that expectation, then you already have a high position. Such a desire will make you become smaller and smaller. Every job is special in its own field. If you go to the hair salon, it is the barber's special job to cut hair. If you go to the dry cleaners, it is the special job of the person there to clean clothes. So every field of work has its own position. The work you do is the work you were destined to do. You should do it with the understanding that it is just your job. All work, no matter what it is, is simply work.

I read a story called "The Lords' Club." This club had a rule that only lords were admitted to the premises. But on the day of the first meeting, when all the lords went inside the club, they felt that they had entered a dark city. There was no one to cook, no one to wait on the tables, no one to wash the cups and saucers. There was nobody to do any work because they were all children of lords. Finally, they had a committee meeting and made a decision. They said, "Since we allow only lords to come here, we will have to do our own work. Otherwise, our club won't be able to function." So they wrote down each job on a piece of paper and put all the pieces in a basket. One said "secretary," one said "guard," one said "cook," one said "president," one said "treasurer," and one said "dishwasher." Each lord drew a lot. One of the greatest lords drew the lot that said "guard," so he went to stand at the door. A second one drew the cook's lot, so he went to the kitchen to prepare tea. A third drew his lot and found that he was supposed to wash the plates. A fourth drew the president's lot. A fifth was the secretary. That day their club went very well. The next Sunday they had the same program. This time the previous president became the guard. The treasurer became the cook. Because of their destiny they had to do their own kind of work. Nonetheless, they were all children of lords, and they all had the feeling that they were the children of lords.

In the same way, we all do different kinds of work, but none of us has a permanent position. One person brings a lot saying that he's a priest. Another person brings a lot saying that she's a dancer. Someone else brings a lot saying that she's a teacher. But all the jobs are transitory and no matter what work we are doing we are all the children of the Lord. This world is the Lord's club. No matter what position we hold, our awareness of being the Lord should never change. The supreme Truth is within every person. Just as the members of that club always remembered that they were lords, in the same way you should remember that you are the supreme Truth. This is man's duty. A person should not think, "I am this," or "I am that." These kinds of feelings are transitory. They are short-lived. When you are playing a certain role, you have a certain name, but it is not the ultimate Truth.

Do not worry about your position; it is the highest.

Competition

Q: What is the right attitude to have when you find yourself competing for a certain job? There are so many talented people.

SM: I feel that to compete for anything is a sign of weakness. Instead of trying to compete, you should increase your own worthiness. That is greatness. When you try to compete with somebody, you are bringing about your own downfall; you are not really going higher. In India there was a great swami who before he became a swami was a great professor of mathematics. His name was Rama Tirth. He was teaching in the MA class, and at that time there was fighting going on among his students. He told them, "You are trying to compete with one another, but that does not make you rise higher." When you try to compete with others, your enthusiasm, your vigor, your great feeling contracts and you feel low.

Professor Rama Tirth drew a line on the blackboard. He told the students, "Make this line shorter." Immediately the students got up. One tried to erase one corner, the other tried to erase the other corner. Rama Tirth said, "Don't touch it; don't hate the line. Without touching it, without any feeling of enmity, try to make it shorter." All the students became quiet; they could not do anything. He asked, "Should I make it shorter without touching it?" He drew another line which was longer than the first line. Then he said, "Didn't I make the first line shorter?"

There's so much space for you to grow. You do not have to put somebody else down in order to go higher.

Become a Witness

Q: My work brings me in contact with many people who are in pain. How can I help these people without becoming involved in their suffering?

SM: A person should work in the mundane world just as an actor or an actress works in a theater. Kashmir Shaivism says that the Self plays all the different roles in this world, and you should understand that everything you are doing is part of the play of the Self. In India a great epic, the *Ramayana*, is performed on the stage. There are two main characters: Rama, the Lord, and Ravana, a demon with ten heads. Ravana is portrayed as a wicked and ferocious creature, and whenever he comes on stage the children shriek, thinking that Ravana himself has actually appeared. But when the curtain is closed, Ravana removes his heads and only the head of the actor remains. Once the play is over the actor becomes his old self. When you are working, just consider yourself to be playing a role. Then you won't be troubled. Keep working and performing actions, but don't identify yourself with your actions. Identify yourself as the witness of the actions, and simply watch everything happen.

Money and Spirituality

Q: There is a geat deal of confusion about money and its relation to spiritual life. Most people are concerned about making more of it, but some people say that you have to give up money, that you have to reduce your needs.

SM: True renunciation of money means using it to help people. You should work, earn money and save it, and help poor people. You should not waste money no matter how prosperous you are. If God has given you wealth, you should take very good care of it. You should respect it.

Q: So having money should not inhibit one in the spiritual search?

SM: It can become an obstacle if you make it an obstacle. We can make anything an obstacle, and we can make anything our friend. A great being said, "Earn money and use it for something good, because God has given you that money."

Right Livelihood

Q: I know quite a few people who are receiving food stamps or unemployment checks from the government. Does one incur karmic debts by accepting food, money, or medical care from the government?

SM: There is no joy in being in debt to anyone. However, each country has its own ways. In India the viewpoint is that a person must not be in debt to anyone. Perhaps in your country people feel differently; perhaps it is considered good for someone who becomes sick to accept money from the government. It won't harm you to accept unemployment checks from the government, but you should spend your time in intense meditation and *japa* and prayer to the Lord; then you won't be incurring any karmic burden. If you accept unemployment checks and don't do any spiritual practice, if instead of putting in hard work in return for the assistance you receive you spend time in lethargy and sloth, then you will only be increasing the weight of your karma.

I read a story about a Sufi saint who sewed hats. Every day he would sew hats and sell them. He lived on the money he made from selling one cap and distributed the money he received from selling the other caps among the poor. He lived a very pure life and spent his time chanting and remembering the Lord. He was also a great Guru, and a great Guru always likes to live by his own labor. One day a man with inherited wealth came to meet this Guru and was profoundly impressed when he saw how he lived, how devoted he was to the Lord, and how pure and sinless he was. The next day he brought the Guru a large amount of money and asked him to distribute it among the poor.

"To whom should I distribute it?" asked the Guru.

"Distribute it to whomever you like," the rich man replied.

So the money was distributed among a group of blind, crippled beggars. Soon after the money had been given out, the Guru asked the benefactor to find the people whom he had helped and learn what they had done with the money. The benefactor had the beggars followed and found that the moment they had received the money they had got a new lease on life, a new rush of energy. One ran to a restaurant and ate greedily, another ran to a dive and let himself go with the women there, while a third got drunk. When the benefactor reported all of this to the Guru, the Guru handed him four coins and asked him to give them away. He said, "You may give these coins to any beggar you encounter. Then go after him and see what he does with them." The rich man left and found a mendicant dressed in rags. He gave the mendicant the four coins, and the mendicant went straight into the forest. There he pulled something from his pocket and threw it away. The rich man, who had followed him into the forest, saw that he had thrown away a dead pigeon. "What were you doing with that?" he asked.

"I have been starving for two days," replied the mendicant. "Today I saw this dead bird on the roadside and picked it up, thinking that I would cook it and fill my stomach. But now I have four coins and can buy my food, so I won't have to eat a dead bird." He went to a stand and bought bread and other things. The rich man returned and reported this to the Guru.

"This is the difference between giving away hard-earned money and money acquired in other ways," the Guru said. "My money is hard-earned; it also has the power of chanting and prayer to the Lord behind it. That is why it was well used."

So it is better to work for your living. Then whatever use your money is put to will bear good fruit. It is my belief that everyone should work for what he eats. If you want your spiritual practice to bear fruit quickly, then you should work for your food; you should eat pure food and eat frugally. If you offer food to the Lord and eat it as His *prasad* while chanting His name, then you will not incur any kind of debt. If you can't find a job, you should at least put in some service. Work hard, earn a lot, and give a part of your earnings to others. Then you will have justified your birth, and you will also find peace.

Alleviating Misery

Q: How does the awareness of the Self in each of us alleviate the misery human beings are facing all over the earth, like war, hunger, and exploitation?

SM: The source of all miseries is lack of knowledge of the Self. Fighting and war go on because we do not know the Self. Once we see the Self in ourselves and others, we can have no more hostility or fear. Of course, knowledge of the Self will not satisfy your hunger for afternoon lunch. Hunger will always be there, and you can satisfy it only by eating food. However, a person who knows the Self becomes more skilled at everything. Through meditation and knowledge of the Self, one can gain knowledge of how to get food.

You should understand that it is the nature of the world to go up and down. Change is the law of nature. Sometimes you are affluent; sometimes you are poor. The world will always be like this. However, the knowledge of the Self will redeem you, will make you overcome all these difficulties.

Nature is constantly creating, sustaining, and destroying all the things of the world. Everything is subject to six modifications. Just as a human being experiences the stages of birth, childhood, youth, maturity, old age, and death, these same six modifications exist in every place, in every country, in every action, and in every religion. Understand this and become calm. These modifications will continue to disturb you as long as you have not attained knowledge of the Self, but after you know the Self, these modifications will no longer bother you. So many things are created and so many things are destroyed. They come into being and they cease to exist. Why does this happen? They are destroyed so that new things can arise, and as the new things arise the old things vanish. In the scriptures there are question and answer sessions. Some are very simple and straightforward, and some are crooked and go around in circles. In one scripture a sage asks, "Why was that man born?" The disciple replies, "To die after a while." "Why did that person die?" "To take birth again in the future."

This is what life in the world is like: things take birth and die, take birth and die. Only That is eternally true; it is all that really exists. When you know this, you remain calm under all circumstances.

Living Through the Drama

Q: How can we protect ourselves from the negativity and grossness that our living and working conditions may expose us to and at the same time see and love the Self behind it all?

SM: The seer Shuka once put a similar question to King Janaka when he was in his court. The king's court was absolutely magnificent. It was full of performing artists, actors, and dancers. Shukamuni was standing in a corner watching it all, fascinated and amazed. King Janaka was sitting in the midst of everything. The king welcomed the young seer. Shuka was held in high esteem in Janaka's time, so the king called him to the throne and asked, "What brings you here, sir?"

Shuka said, "Your majesty, this world is full of inequality and disharmony, and when I see it my heart is full of pain. In one place a new child is born, while somewhere else someone dies. One person is dancing while another is weeping. Some people are making merry while others are depressed. I have heard that you have attained equality-consciousness and that you are established in a state beyond body-consciousness. What is the secret? How can you remain unaffected even while seeing all this inequality and experiencing all this disharmony? Please explain this to me very clearly so that it will sink into me."

The king said, "I will explain it to you tomorrow in a very concrete way. You will realize the truth of what I tell you through direct experience."

The next day the king ordered all the festivities that were usually held in the court to be held in the main street of the capital. When Shuka came to the court, the king ordered a dish of water to be placed on his head. Though Shuka's head was already shaved, he was given a fresh shave, and the dish was put on his head. Then the king ordered four armed sentries to serve as his escorts. He said, "As he goes through the capital, if even a single drop of water falls from the dish, cut off his head. Don't show the least pity; just cut off his head on the spot."

When Shuka heard these orders, he wondered whether he had acted intelligently in putting his question to such a man. But nothing could be done. Shuka was quite intelligent and discreet. He accepted the situation and walked through the main street with the dish of water on his head. He made sure that not a single drop fell from it. Then he returned to the palace. He put the dish of water down. Seeing that not a single drop had fallen and that Shuka was still alive, the king honored him. Then he asked, "Holy sir, did you watch the festivities that were going on in the main street—the acting of the actors, the dancing of the dancers, and the other things?"

"No, not at all," Shuka said. "My mind was fastened on the dish of water on my head the whole time, because I knew that if even a single drop fell, I would be no more. So that was where my attention was focused. No festivity could distract me."

This is exactly how we should conduct ourselves in the world. All kinds of things happen in the outside world. We should watch them with witness-consciousness, without being affected. Our minds should always be focused on the *sahasrara*.

The world is full of change and inequality. If there is progress in one direction, there is decline in another. Increase in one field is always balanced by decrease in another field. If you find people enjoying more individual freedom, you also find them losing their health. If you find wealth increasing in one nation, you also find morality declining. This is what goes on, and this will always go on. There is really nothing in this world that should amuse you or make you sad. The world is nothing but a play, a sport. It would become monotonous if it stayed the same. A play is constantly changing. A wise person realizes this truth and remains unaffected. Only if we lack discrimination, only if we do not think correctly about things do we fail to understand that in order for the drama of this world to go on there have to be opposing forces. A single force could not sustain the drama. It was only because Rama was opposed by Ravana that we had the play of the *Ramayana*. It was because Duryodhana existed along with Yudhisthira and Bhishma that we had the play of the *Mahabharata*.

There will always be inequality in the universe. There will always be opposing forces. Realizing this truth, a wise person remains unaffected. The world will always remain as it is. Sometimes it seems to progress, and other times it seems to decline. You should keep your mind fixed on the *sahasrara*.

The Inner and the Outer

Q: When we work on our inner environment by chanting and meditating, do we affect our outer environment?

SM: A person's feelings and thoughts definitely affect the outer environment. In the great epic the *Tulsi Ramayana*, there is the story of Kakabhushundi, who constantly repeated God's name. The effect of this repetition spread everywhere within two miles of where Kakabhushundi lived. Whoever came into that area would automatically start repeating God's name. Lord Buddha observed nonviolence. His belief and his practice affected the atmosphere around him so much that when animals who were natural enemies came into his presence, they would give up their enmity and sit very quietly together. Mahatma Gandhi was a believer in the truth. If a thief appeared before him, he would automatically confess his crimes. Even if he might be running from the police, he wouldn't be able to lie in front of Mahatma Gandhi. So a person's inner feelings and actions not only affect him inside, but also affect the atmosphere around him.

There are one thousand people living in my ashram. They rarely have to visit doctors because chanting and the repetition of God's name make them strong and healthy. When you create this kind of atmosphere, it has its own power. That is why a person should always have sublime feelings in his heart. A person's feeling has great power. If one person leads a life full of love and respect, it affects the lives of many others, because everything in this world is totally related to everything else. Our actions also affect nature.

Since it is Consciousness alone that exists in everything, it is very natural that everything should be interrelated. Without the earth, water cannot exist; without water, the earth cannot exist. Without air, fire cannot exist; without fire, air cannot exist. The same close relationship that exists between you and other people also exists between you and nature. If it is hot outside you feel hot inside. If it is cold outside you feel cold inside. Whatever nature feels is what you feel. But most of us do not understand this, and therefore we do not realize that whatever we do affects nature. Our bad actions as well as our good ones are reflected in the environment around us. That is why, in ancient India, elaborate fire rituals used to be held to please the forces controlling rain, fire, and fertility. In those days, those forces bestowed their gifts abundantly on the land. Now such rituals are no longer performed, and these forces, too, seem to have slackened in their functions. The way in which we treat nature is reflected in her behavior toward us. It is because we treat nature and our fellow beings without respect that so many natural catastrophes are occurring in the world today.

Helping Others

Q: What can people who are inspired to work for the good of society do to help improve our deteriorating environment?

SM: Before trying to help others, every individual should first improve the way he leads his or her own life. I meet many people who are trying to improve others but who haven't yet improved themselves. Many tell me, "I want to offer my service to the world," but when I ask about their own condition, I find that it is terrible. Without first becoming a doctor, how can you help patients? If you have no money in the bank, how can you loan money to others? Before trying to serve society, people should first uplift themselves. Then they will be able to offer their service to the world in a real way.

If everyone learned to look upon others with respect and to truly welcome others, that would be a tremendous help to the world.

Political Action

Q: It seems to me that fulfilling our responsibility to our fellow beings involves some political action. Could you comment on this?

SM: There will always be conflicts, because that is the nature of the world, and no matter what system of government prevails in a country, the enforcement of law will always involve a certain amount of repression. If you want to do something in the political field, you are welcome to. But remember, the people who oppose you are human beings just as you are. One who is your friend today may become your enemy tomorrow, and one who is your enemy today may become your friend the day after. It is good to work toward improving the world through political action, provided that you look upon the people involved with the right attitude, which is to honor them and to love the Self in them.

The World Is a University

Q: When we find ourselves in a difficult situation, how should we decide whether to persevere because there is a lesson to be learned or whether to get out of the situation because it is not conducive to spiritual growth?

SM: If you get caught in a difficult situation, you shouldn't run away from it. Face it bravely. There is a lesson to be learned in every situation. The world is a huge university, and you can learn everything there. You can learn how to become sick and diseased, and through yoga you can also learn how to become healthy and happy.

In my youth I wandered the length and breadth of India. In those days I didn't beg for food from anyone. I accepted food only if someone offered it to me. On many occasions I wasn't offered any food, so I would dissolve mud in water and then filter and drink it. Sometimes I would even eat mud, yet I did not become dejected. I never lamented; I never wept. I ate clay with courage; I persevered. The result is that now thousands of people are fed every day at my ashram. Nor did I beg for cloth. Sometimes on cold nights when I had nothing to cover my body with, I would go to the shrine of a saint. A long sheet was spread over the shrine, and I would wrap myself with that sheet. In the morning I would rise early, put the sheet back on the shrine, and walk away. The result is that now I have such an abundance of cloth that I am able to give away clothes to the needy.

Face difficult situations with great determination and with great courage. Don't be frightened; seek God's help.

Yoga in the World

Q: Will I be able to engage myself successfully in yogic *sadhana* while having mundane desires and trying to fulfill them? If so, how?

SM: Just as you have mundane desires and spend your time in mundane activities, in the same way you should spend some time doing yoga *sadhana*. Then your mundane life and your spiritual life will grow together. First of all, understand the foundation of yoga very well, and understand worldly life, too. Even though you are leading a worldly life, still I think you don't really understand it; you are just leading it. If you understand the foundation of yoga completely and then look at the world, you will understand that the world is filled with yoga. Yoga is hidden in the world. However, we don't know this. One of the practices of yoga is to sit in one position comfortably for a long time. This is called *asana*. When you are working in the office, don't you sit in one position for a long time? When women cook at home and when they feed their children, don't they sit in one position for a long time? That is also a part of yoga. Do you think that only breathing exercises are yoga? Another part of yoga is meditation. In the world everybody meditates; without meditation you cannot live in the world. You are listening to me one-pointedly, aren't you? To read or listen to something with great attention, with one-pointedness, is also called meditation. You drive your car to the office and your mind is concentrated on which route you should take. This is meditation on driving; still, it is meditation. When you are doing mathematics, you are meditating; when you are cooking, you are meditating. Even when you are accumulating possessions, you are meditating. Modern young boys and girls go to the movies at night and go home remembering the clothes of the actors and actresses so well that in the morning they have the whole picture in their mind. Then they go to a tailor and tell him exactly how they want their clothes made. Maybe they are meditating on a fad, but still they are meditating; the only difference between their meditation and ours is that our meditation is on spirituality. No matter what action you are engaged in, no matter what country you go to, no matter what place you go to, you always remember who you are; you never forget it. You don't need a meter to remind you of yourself and your individuality. So in a sense you are always remembering the Self.

In this way, even in the world there is so much meditation. Maybe it is meditation of the world, but still, if you make these forms of meditation more disciplined and become aware of them, then you will realize that your life is yoga. If you sit quietly, you will find out that your breath is going out and coming in rhythmically. Then you will know that *pranayama* is taking place spontaneously within you. Understand the world; understand that yoga is in your life. Understand yoga completely too, and then you will be able to lead your mundane life and yogic life together. A great being said that a yogi experiences yoga and this world as being the same. Eat more regularly, drink more regularly, follow discipline, say good and pure things, and always speak the truth. If you do this you will be following a part of yoga. Do not misunderstand the world. Do not think that the world is worthless. Do not decrease its value. The world is a beautiful thing that God has created for His own joy. Why do you find unhappiness in it? If there were no joy in this world, then God would not have created it with so much love and effort. So there is some mistake in your understanding and in your behavior—that is why when you look at the world you see unhappiness. So improve your vision, and then you will understand that the world is God.

7

Love

The Love of the Inner Self

Love is our only reason for living and the only purpose of life. We live for the sake of love, and we live seeking love. For the sake of love an actor performs, and for the sake of love a writer writes. For the sake of love a sensualist enjoys the pleasures of the body, and for the sake of love a meditator turns within and isolates himself from the world. Everything we do in life we do with the hope of experiencing love. We say, "If I do not find it today, perhaps I will find it tomorrow. If I do not find it in this person, perhaps I will find it in that one." Love is essential for all of us.

It is not surprising that we keep looking for love, because we are all born of love. We come out of love. All of us are nothing but vibrations of love. We are sustained by love, and in the end we merge into love. In the beginning there was only emptiness. Then God's love began to throb, and everything came into existence. When the love of a husband and wife is expressed, it takes birth in the form of a child. In the same way, according to the great scriptural authors, when the ocean of love of Shiva and Shakti, the supreme Reality and His creative power, overflowed, it took birth as this world and all the creatures in it. So the world is an expansion of God's love and, like Him, it is full of love. This world is nothing but a school of love; our relationships with our husband or wife, with our children and parents, with our friends and relatives are the university in which we are meant to learn what love and devotion truly are.

Yet the love we experience through other people is just a shadow of the love of the inner Self. There is a sublime place inside us where love dwells. Just as electric bulbs derive their power from a power plant, all the love we experience comes from that inner source. Only because that love exists within us are we able to love our friends, our families, our parents, and our children. Even our everyday experience shows us that the real abode of love is within. When two lovers embrace after a long separation, they close their eyes and go inside themselves. They tap that inner source, and then they experience the welling up of love. But once they stop embracing, they come out of themselves and their joy begins to ebb. When they see each other the next day, that intense joy is gone. That is why, if we want to experience complete love, we must plunge within to the place that is its source. That is why we meditate. Through meditation the inner love is unfolded. As we constantly meditate, we get drunk on this inner love, and that is when we begin to realize what love really is.

The love that pulses in the cave of the heart does not depend on anything outside. It does not arise because of the friction of two bodies. It does not expect anything. It is completely independent. Most of the time the mundane love we experience is not love at all, but business. We love each other for the sake of self-interest, but as soon as our desires are fulfilled we no longer belong to one another.

Once in India there was a great king called Bhartrihari. In his kingdom lived a saint who spent all of his time in ascetic practices. As a result of his *tapasya*, he had acquired a great boon, the fruit of immortality. When this fruit came into his hands, he thought, "What use would it be to anyone if I became immortal? The king is so great. If I were to give this fruit to him, he would continue to rule in justice forever and the land would always be in peace." Immediately the saint went to Bhartrihari's court and handed the fruit to the king. Now the king loved his wife, whose name was Pingala, very dearly. He could not stand the thought of living without her. As soon as he received the fruit he began to think, "It would be very good if Pingala were to eat this fruit and become immortal; then as long as I lived I would never be afraid of losing her!" Bhartrihari gave the fruit to Pingala, but Pingala had a boyfriend whom she loved very much. I am telling you about the ways of what is called love. Pingala thought to herself, "If my boyfriend became immortal, I would never lose him." So she gave the fruit to him. The queen's boyfriend had a girlfriend, who was a courtesan. He loved her very much and wanted her to become immortal, so he passed the fruit on to her. The courtesan was a very ordinary woman; she thought to herself, "I am of no use to anyone. I am such a sinful person. Why should I become immortal? But the king is such a benevolent ruler. If he were to live forever, that would benefit the whole kingdom." So she went to the king and handed him the fruit. "Your majesty," she said, "this is the fruit of immortality. Please eat it and may your subjects prosper and be happy under you." The king was shocked. The moment he saw the fruit he realized what had been happening. He said, "Love has gone full circle and come back to me." His eyes were opened, and he understood the futility of worldly love. He renounced his throne and became a great saint.

True love, the love that springs from the Self, is not like this mundane love. The love of the Self is selfless and unconditional. It is not relative. It is completely free. It is self-generated and it never dies. This kind of love knows no distinction between high and low, between man and woman. Just as the earth remains the same no matter who comes and goes on it, so true love remains unchanging and independent. Love penetrates your entire being. Love is Consciousness. Love is bliss. It does not exist for the sake of .omething else. It is supremely free. The path of this inner love leads a lover to God. As a person walks on that path he not only attains love, but merges in the ocean of love.

The path of love is called *bhakti* yoga. Every spiritual path has its own scripture which explains it. The great scripture of love is the *Bhakti Sutras* of Maharishi Narada. In the *Bhakti Sutras*, Narada discusses the nature of the inner divine love. He says that this inner love cannot be described. When a person drinks it, he attains a state that is beyond words. Then he is like a dumb person trying to describe the taste of sugar; all that he can say is, "Aah, aah." When such a lover becomes saturated with love, his mind, intellect, and ego are stilled. He becomes silent and takes delight in the inner Self. Narada says, "One who attains divine love becomes serene and satisfied within himself." That inner love is so delicious that one who tastes it becomes completely fulfilled. Such a being loses all his desires. Through the power of love, all the great Siddhas were able to bring their senses completely under their control. The senses want joy, and to find it they turn outward. But once the love of the inner Self begins welling up, why should the senses give up this fountain of nectar and go out looking for saltwater? The great sage Shukamuni said, "One who constantly swims in the ocean of divine love will not take interest in rivers and streams." A being who is experiencing that inner love has no desires. He does not need to look for outer pleasures. He has no desire to go to different places or to exercise different talents and skills. Everything has been fulfilled for him. He becomes completely free of anxiety and fear. He never wonders, "What will happen to me tomorrow?" He neither worries nor becomes excited. He no longer feels attached to anything, nor does he hate anything.

The poet Tulsidas was a yogi of love. He said, "When a person attains the love of the Self, love pours from his eyes and he sees his own beloved everywhere." When this is the case, how can he hate anybody? Another great yogi of love said, "Once God began to pervade my heart, once love welled up inside, I began to see love in trees, in branches, in flowers."

To have complete love for God is a great *sadhana*. There was a great poet-saint in our country who sang of devotion in his poetry. In one of his verses he says, "O Mother Bhakti, you are so full of Shakti. In one of your hands you hold liberation, and in the other you hold the wealth and pleasures of this world. You fill our hearts with love and bliss. O Mother Devotion, you have boundless power. You make a poor man rich, a beggar a king; you fulfill the fondest desires of a wretched man, and you make a mere king a supreme sovereign. You reveal the reality which lies behind unreality, the consciousness in matter. You fill our hearts at all times." This is the greatness of the path of love.

Among all types of *sadhana*, *bhakti* is the easiest—still, it is very difficult to follow. Devotees who practice *bhakti* yoga worship a particular form of God and, through that worship, eventually reach that God who is formless and who is the Self. However, the *Vijnana Bhairava* says that true *bhakti* does not mean going to a temple or a mosque and praying to God outside oneself. True *bhakti* is knowing the Lord who pervades everything equally in the form of being, consciousness, and bliss absolute.

The Gopis had this kind of love. Their love was mysterious and astounding. It was so great that Narada and other great sages used it as an example of the highest devotion. The Gopis were all householders in the town of Vrindavan. They never left their homes;

they never renounced their families, their children, or their household activities. Even while living in the world and performing their worldly activities they were able to manifest the most complete love for God. When a person truly loves God, her worldly life does not suffer; it improves. Only a person who loves God can truly love her husband, her children, and her society; she can love the entire world.

Lord Krishna lived among the Gopis for many years, but eventually he had to leave them. He traveled from one city to another, and wherever he went many sages and devotees surrounded him. One of the Lord's great disciples was Uddhava. Uddhava had mastered all branches of knowledge, he had practiced every aspect of yoga, and he had performed many austerities. Because he was so great and because he knew so much, it was natural for him to have a big ego. Ego is the enemy of love. Narada said, "If you want to experience devotion, you must give up ego and pretension." If you keep these things inside your heart, there will be no room for God.

Not only was Krishna the Lord; he was also the Guru. So he possessed the skill of teaching someone in a way that was perfectly suited to him. The Lord looked at Uddhava and said to himself, "He is very intelligent. He is a great scholar and teacher, and he knows all about yoga. But because of his ego his heart is dry. Unless his ego leaves him, he will not be able to experience love." One day Krishna said, "O Uddhava, you are a great man of knowledge and you are very dear to me. Now I need your help."

When Uddhava heard these words, his ego swelled even more. "Of course, Lord," he said. "I will do anything you ask."

Krishna said, "A long time ago I left the Gopis in Vrindavan. They love me very much, and I am afraid they must miss me. I want you to go to Vrindavan and give them news of me. Then I want you to teach them yoga, knowledge, and meditation and bring peace to their hearts. Tell them that I am doing very well and that if they meditate and practice yoga they will also be happy."

Uddhava was very happy. The Gopis were considered to be great beings, and if the Lord had appointed him to teach them, what a high state he must have attained! With great speed he traveled to Vrindavan and stood on the bank of the Yamuna River. There he observed the condition of the Gopis. They were so immersed in their love for Krishna that they had lost themselves completely.

They would go about their daily activities, but as they dipped their water pots in the river they would look at the water and say, "Hai, Krishna." As they walked up the bank, they would embrace the trees and say, "Hai, Krishna!" When they milked the cows, they would embrace the calves and say, "Hai, Krishna!" When they saw one another, they would embrace and say, "Hai, Krishna!" As Uddhava watched them, he thought to himself, "These women are maniacs. They have gone completely crazy. They are so deluded that they are seeing Krishna everywhere."

Uddhava hailed the Gopis, and they came running. They surrounded him and embraced him. Devotees always welcome another devotee, especially one who has come directly from the Lord.

"How is the Lord?" they asked him.

"He is happy, and he sends you all his love," Uddhava said. "He thought that you must all be depressed without him, so he sent me here to help you out of your condition. Sit down and listen to me."

The Gopis sat around Uddhava, and then he began to speak. "You are all deluded," he said. "You look at the river and call it Krishna. You look at a calf and call it Krishna. You embrace a tree and say, 'Hai, Krishna.' This behavior is crazy. Listen very carefully. Yoga has eight limbs, and from now on you should practice them. You should sit for meditation and withdraw your consciousness into the heart. In the heart there is a lotus, and Krishna can be seen there. If you meditate you will experience him within, and you will find peace."

The Gopis listened very politely to Uddhava. Narada said that even though the Gopis were so intoxicated, they did not lack understanding. They had not lost their power of memory, nor had they lost their decorum. They had complete knowledge of everything. When Uddhava had finished explaining yoga to them, the Gopis said, "O Uddhava, your yoga and your knowledge are of no use to us. We cannot follow them; we cannot even understand them. We have only one mind, and that mind has gone to Krishna. With what mind are we going to practice your yoga and your knowledge? What are we going to see in meditation? O Uddhava, the Lord permeates our entire being from head to toe. The Lord is in our mind. The Lord is in our breath. We see Krishna in the trees, in the river, in the sky, in the clouds. All we see, whether animate or inanimate, is Krishna. Wherever we look, we see Krishna."

As Uddhava listened to the Gopis, he became silent and humble. He realized that through their devotion to Krishna they had attained the state of complete unity-awareness. This was the greatness of the Gopis. In their husbands they saw Krishna, in their children they saw Krishna, and in their cows they saw Krishna. They saw Krishna in everything and performed their activities with the awareness that Krishna was in all. Their devotion was nondual; it permeated everything.

If you have this kind of love, God reveals Himself in every pore of your body. When you experience God within, you become aware that the same God exists in everyone. Then you begin to worship that God in all.

A person who is immersed in love does not have to keep saying "I love you" to express his feelings. Just as the fragrance of a flower spreads naturally and everyone who passes by enjoys it, so the love of such a lover spreads to everyone who comes into contact with him. Great beings such as Mirabai, Tulsidas, Namdev, and Jesus were soaked in love, and whoever stayed in their company became infected with it. A person who only gives and takes in the name of love is simply imitating the love of those beings who were the embodiment of love.

If you want to attain this sort of love you have to become love. You have to be saturated with love. You have to discard your small "I"-awareness, the idea that you are a man or a woman or an intelligent person or a fool. The gates of love will never open for one whose love is contaminated with false identification.

Once there was a temple of love. Someone went to the door and knocked. A voice inside asked, "Who are you?"

"I am a philosopher."

"There is no place in this temple for a philosopher," said the voice. "You had better go to a university and teach there."

Then another person knocked on the door, and the same voice asked, "Who are you?"

"I am a religious teacher."

"Why do we need a religious teacher here? You had better go

somewhere else and deceive the people there with all your teachings."

A third person knocked, and the voice asked, "Who are you?"

"A hatha yogi."

"What do we need a hatha yogi for? Where hatha yoga ends, love begins. Go away."

A fourth person came, and again the voice asked, "Who are you?"

"I am an intellectual; I examine everything with my penetrating intellect."

"What do we need your intellectual games here for? When the intellect becomes bewildered and reaches the end of its cleverness, love begins."

Then a fifth person came and knocked on the door. He knocked hard, and the voice within asked, "Who are you?"

"I am a great seeker; I am the great disciple of a great Guru."

"Go away immediately," said the voice. "We don't need the disciple of a great Guru here."

Another person knocked. "Who are you?" the voice asked.

"I am I."

"Why have you brought your 'I' here? Of what use will your 'I' be in this place?"

Another person knocked. "Who are you?" the voice asked.

"Hunh."

"Who are you?"

"Hunh."

The gate was opened, and the person at the door was allowed to enter the temple of love.

To find the love of the Self you have to leave everything behind. If you carry any burden on your heart, you cannot attain the inner love. You have to rid yourself of ego. Only then can you experience that love. When you become immersed in love, you become one with love. You merge in the ocean of love. In the *Shrimad Bhagavatam* there is a story about Radha. Radha was so devoted to Krishna that she thought of nothing else. Finally, she became so immersed in Krishna that she became Krishna and began to ask her friends, "Where is Radha?" She had lost herself completely in love. In the same way, you must lose yourself in the Self. When you become one with the inner love, that love will saturate your entire being and you yourself will become the embodiment of love.

How to Experience Love

If you want to experience love, you have to start by loving yourself. First you have to love your body, then those who are related to your body, and then the master of the body, the inner Self.

You must understand the value of this body and then make it strong through hatha yoga, meditation, and chanting God's name. This body is your greatest friend, and treachery against a friend is not good. Feed your body regularly and with self-control. Take good care of it; make it an abode fit for God to live in. Then love all those who are related to your body: your mother, father, brothers, sisters, friends, relatives, husband or wife, and children. That is how love expands.

The truth is that God has no physical body; the only body He has is the body of love. If the love you experience in your daily life—the little love you feel for your friends, your relatives, your pets, and even your possessions—could be turned toward the inner Self, that would be enough to bring you liberation.

Teaching the Mind

Q: You once told me to teach my mind to love myself. What is the best way for me to do this?

SM: Question your mind. Ask your mind whether it finds happiness in fickleness or in stillness. Tell your mind that it has been wandering here and there according to its own whim without finding anything or attaining anything. Tell it that for this reason it should try to enter the Self. Teach the mind good things about your Self. Talk to the mind about the love of your own Self. Then you will experience that love.

Reason Has No Value

To follow the path of love you do not need any outer qualifications. You do not have to be beautiful or come from an important family. You do not have to be well educated. You do not need degrees or money. Even the simplest person can experience the sweetness of love.

Once the Sufi Hasrat Mussa was walking through a field when he heard a peasant praying to God. The peasant was saying, "O Lord, O master of the universe, O controller of all, please come to my hut and stay with me just for a few days. I will give You my bed to sleep in, and I'll cover You with my quilt. I'll massage Your feet and make delicious porridge for You. O Lord, I will take such good care of You."

Mussa thought, "This man must be crazy. After all, God is without attribute; He has no form. What made this man think that God is like a human being who will come and lie down on a bed?" Mussa stood in front of the peasant and yelled at him, "What are you doing?"

"I'm praying to God," the peasant answered.

"And what are you saying?"

"I am asking God to come and stay in my house for a few days."

Mussa said, "You have committed a great sin. God is not a human being. He does not have a physical body. He neither eats nor drinks, nor sleeps, nor gives, nor takes, and He certainly does not visit people's houses. You have insulted Him!"

The peasant was a very simple man, and when he heard this he held his earlobes and said, "O Lord, forgive me, forgive me. I'll never do it again."

Mussa went home, and in the evening he sat down to pray. As soon as he closed his eyes, a voice from the heavens said, "O Mussa, you have committed the most terrible sin. I sent you into this world on a special mission. I sent you here to turn people's hearts toward Me, but you are turning hearts that have already turned toward Me away!"

Next to love, reason has no value.

Laila and Majunu

I will tell you a story about love. Laila was the daughter of a king, and Majunu was the son of the king's washerman. Every day Majunu's father washed the king's clothes and returned them to the palace. However, one day he was so busy that he asked Majunu to return the clothes. The king's maids were also busy, so Laila went to the door to take the clothes from Majunu. The ways of karma are strange. She was a princess; of course, she was very beautiful. What can you say after that? The beauty of a woman is the beauty of God. It really bewitches you. The moment Majunu saw the princess he was lost. He gave the clothes to her, and that was that. The guards had to pick him up and throw him out.

When he left the palace, Majunu began to wander around the town crying, "Laila, Laila, Laila." He could see only Laila everywhere. He became so absorbed in love for her that nothing else could enter his mind. He forgot to eat and drink. He went around like a mad person, lost in his love for Laila. His friends and family tried to reason with him, but he would not listen to anybody.

This is the state of true love. If you don't love your inner Self like this, then you are not a true lover. If you just close your eyes for a minute and then open them, it is not true love.

Finally, the king was told about Majunu's predicament. He was told, "Majunu doesn't eat; he doesn't drink. All that he does is say, 'Laila, Laila, Laila.'"

The king took pity on Majunu. He issued an order that all the restaurant owners in the capital should give him food, and that the merchants should provide him with clothes and shoes. They were told to give Majunu whatever he needed and to send the bills to the palace.

Now everyone in that place was very selfish. The only one who wasn't selfish was the one who had lost himself in love. In this world everybody has his self-interest. Once a person's self-interest is fulfilled, then the wife doesn't belong to the husband and the husband doesn't belong to the wife. Everyone belongs to his own self-interest.

There were some idle young men of the town who began to watch what was happening. They thought to themselves, "Being Majunu is a good deal. You don't have to go to all the trouble of working. You can go to any shop and get whatever you want for free." One day, four or five Majunus appeared on the street, all of them crying, "Laila, Laila, Laila." The restaurant owners and the clothing merchants were delighted to give them food and clothes and to send the bills to the palace. Seeing this, more men came, and they too began to clap and say, "Laila, Laila, Laila." After a while the bills became so enormous that the king finally called his prime minister and asked him, "What's going on? There is only one Majunu, but millions of dollars are being spent!"

"Your Majesty," replied the prime minister, "leave the matter to me." The prime minister called all the town criers and told them to go around the town beating their drums and announcing that on the following day at noon Majunu would be hanged. As soon as they heard this, all the Majunus stopped crying, "Laila, Laila, Laila," and ran away to save their lives. Just one Majunu remained. He did not care about his life, nor did he care about his death. All that he cared about was Laila, and he still continued to cry out her name.

This is true love. If a person is filled with love, then he can see only his beloved everywhere. Majunu had become so engrossed in love that he no longer needed an external Laila. Everything had become Laila for him. When he was eating, the food was Laila. When he was drinking, the water was Laila. All of the objects of his senses had become Laila. One day he was searching through a heap of garbage. Someone asked him, "O Majunu, what are you doing?" He said, "I am looking for Laila."

The power of real love is very great. Because Majunu was in such a state of love, Laila began to feel that love, too. Even though they had not seen one another since their first meeting, Laila began to wander through the palace crying out, "Majunu, Majunu, Majunu." The king tried to distract her, but whenever he suggested going to the theater, all that she could say was, "Will Majunu be there?" If he proposed a trip to the country, all that she could say was, "Will Majunu be there?" Finally, the king realized that there was no point in keeping the lovers separated. He gave his daughter to Majunu. Because of his great love, Majunu attained his Laila.

If you want to find God, love Him madly; if you want to experience the Self, love it madly. Lose yourself in love. Do not hold yourself back. Then you will attain your beloved.

The Love That Springs from Within

Q: During meditation I experience lots of energy and thoughts in my head. What can I do to connect my head with my heart and experience the love that seems locked up inside? Is this love the experience of the inner Self?

SM: Yes, this love is the experience of the inner Self. It is not only the love that wells up in your heart during meditation that is the love of the inner Self. Whatever you do in your daily activities, if you experience love while you are laughing, when you meet your friends, while you are eating, when you enjoy your food, even that is the love of the inner Self. Not only that, if you experience a lot of love while taking a bath, even that is the love of the inner Self. However, when you depend on the love emanating from these things, it is only temporary. Love should well up within you without depending on anything, without any cause. That is the true love.

Since time immemorial people in the world have spent their entire lives loving each other. Two people love each other intensely, but neither loves himself in the same way. When two people are in love, what happens? The lover projects the love of his own heart, the love that is inside him, onto his beloved, and he experiences satisfaction and happiness as a result. The beloved does the same; she projects her own love onto her lover and experiences satisfaction and happiness. But that is not what Vedanta or yoga teaches. Vedanta says that you should continuously focus the love within you on your own inner Self and find your happiness, your joy, right within your own heart, not in someone else. Otherwise, you project the love within you onto another individual and think that your own happiness and joy are coming from that individual.

The love you receive from another person does not last. It waxes and wanes; it depends on the other person. It is not a reliable support; it is feeble and temporary. You should experience the love that is in your own heart. Try to make your own love arise from your inner depths. Then you will know what true love, true bliss, is. The moment you become saturated with the love that springs from within, that love will flow toward every object you see. Then you will not have to make an effort to love another person. You will not have to indulge in all the hysterics that you call love. You will not have to cry or shout at the top of your voice, "I love you, I love you, and my love is true." That is nothing but a melodramatic theatrical performance. It is not the real thing. It is only when you begin to love yourself that you will know what love is. These play-actors of love swear in the name of God, in the name of every other deity, that their love is true, but it remains utter falsehood.

You know from your own experience that whenever anger arises within you, it pours out onto whomever comes in contact with you, regardless of whether that person is dear to you or a stranger. When anger flows out of you toward others in such a natural manner, why won't love? If it has been released in your heart, why won't it flow toward others? Then you will not have to make protestations of love. You will not have to swear. You will not have to convince the other person that your love is true. Your love will flow out in a natural way.

The Source of Love

Q: What is the source of your love? How do you manage to love everyone all the time?

SM: I continue to love my own Self. As I increase my love for my own Self, my joy permeates everybody. For example, if you are sad and weeping, if you are feeling pitiful, others automatically start weeping with you. You do not have to tell them, "Start crying with me." In the same way, I continue to laugh with joy, and you catch that feeling spontaneously and start laughing, too. Express joy on your face, and you will see another person do the same. I look at everyone with joy. This vision of joy is great.

Love Without Attachment

Q: How can I love another person without forming an attachment to him?

SM: If you give up attachment, you will not have to make an effort to love, because very naturally you will experience the love that always exists within you. It is attachment which obscures that real love. As soon as you give up attachment, pure love will reveal itself to you. You should become detached from others and attached to your own Self. Then the independent love of the Self will reveal itself to you.

Annihilation

Q: No matter how hard I try to open myself to other people, I still am not loving enough. I want so much to do this but cannot. Can you help me?

SM: If you really want to love others, if you really want to help them, first you should efface yourself; you should destroy the petty ego that separates you from others and from God. That is why Mansur Mastana said, "Totally annihilate yourself if you want to acquire divinity." Unless you efface yourself, you will never be able to find God. It is only when a seed has annihilated itself in the soil that it grows and produces beautiful flowers and fruit. In the same way, it is only when you discard your limited ego that you will be able to truly love.

No Separation

Q: Baba, I want to love you but I feel separate from you. What can I do?

SM: You try to love me. That is what separates you from me. If a person wants to love someone but thinks that person is separate from him, he cannot love that person. When the love of the Self arises within you through knowledge and meditation, you will realize that the same love is in everything and in everyone. A great being said, "O Lord, You are me and I am You. This is my worship." Whoever truly loves others loves them with the awareness that they are his own Self. Even if he loves another person, he loves that person for his own sake because it is he who feels that love.

Yajnavalkya, the great sage, told his wife, "O Maitreyi, I love you for my own sake, not for your sake. The reason I love you is because I feel that love within me."

I, too, love you for my own sake, not for your sake. Truly speaking, I love my own Self. I have not yet learned how to love others. In my philosophy this wisdom is not taught. I teach a person how to love his or her own Self. So if you want to love me, you should love your own Self. That is the only way your love will reach me.

8

The
Natural
State

The Inner Ecstasy

In the ninth chapter of the *Kularnava Tantra*, it is said, "The best state is the natural state." The scripture goes on to describe three other states. In the second state one practices concentration and meditation. In the third one does *japa* and praises God's glory. In the fourth state one goes on pilgrimages. Of all these, the natural state is the greatest. In that state there is no attachment, no aversion, no anger, and no ego. In that state one naturally maintains the awareness of "I am That." Compared with this awareness, all other practices, such as meditation, *japa*, and repeating the mantra, are mediocre.

It is said that worshipping God a thousand times is as good as repeating a hymn once. Repeating a thousand hymns is equal to one repetition of the mantra. Repeating the mantra a million times is equal to one moment of the total stillness of good meditation. Meditating a million times is equal to one total merging in the Self. Therefore, the scriptures say that to lose oneself in the Self is the true repetition of mantra. There is no greater worship than the worship of the inner Self. There is no greater deity than the Self. A person should consider his own inner Self the Deity and should remain in this natural state all the time.

The natural state is a state of complete stillness and satisfaction. The senses dwell in the senses. They are quiet within themselves. The hands are quiet within themselves. The mind is satisfied within itself. Everything is completely serene and free of action. That is the greatest worship. For the mind to observe silence is the true *japa*, the true mantra repetition. The highest meditation is the thought-free state. Many people complain to me, saying, "In my meditation I don't see anything." But why do you want to see something in your meditation? Wouldn't it be much easier to watch cars moving on the road or planes flying in the sky? So many things happen in this world. Why don't you watch them if you really want to see something? The highest meditation is the state completely free of thoughts and images.

As long as the mind exists, it is constantly brooding. When it stops, when there is no thought and no imagination, that is when a person attains something. There are many sects, many paths, many techniques, but no matter what technique you follow, if the mind remains alive, then it is worldly. It does not matter whether you are following spiritual practices or worldly practices. It does not matter whether you are contemplating Rama or Allah, because whatever the mind can think about remains confined to the mind. Only when the mind becomes free of thoughts, only when it becomes devoid of imagination, only when it loses itself in the Self, do you attain something.

Jnaneshwar Maharaj said, "As your mind contemplates continuously, it stops. Pursue whatever is left. That is the attainment."

A person should stop wasting his time looking for That in one course after another, in one country after another, in one technique after another, in one path after another. There is no point in it. Once Sheikh Nasrudin began to think and think and brood and brood, until he became a half-mental case. This is what happens when you think too much. The mind wears out. When a car is overused, the tires and the engine wear out. So it is not surprising if the mind which thinks too much should also wear out. Nasrudin's mind had become worn out from too much thinking, and he had lost the power of memory. Somebody came to his town and said that he was giving a course to increase people's memory. When Nasrudin heard about the course, he rushed to sign up for it. At the end of the first course, he had not regained his memory; so he took a second one and then a third one. After taking three courses, he gave up. People asked him, "Sheikh Nasrudin, how was your course?"

He said, "Very successful. Now I remember that I forget."

There is no point in taking such courses. Instead, a person should look for That within himself. Inside, there is such great Shakti. There is such a great state, such great intoxication, such great power. For this reason, you should become immersed within yourself. You can attain everything within yourself. You can perceive everything within yourself. There is nothing that is other than your own Self. If you change your attitude and it becomes sublime, you can see God even in a pillar. But if you have a bad attitude, then even God becomes an inert object for you. When you have a bad attitude, you can see hell in this world of Consciousness. When you have a good attitude, you can see Consciousness even in hell.

Whatever is inside you is inside me, and whatever is inside me is inside you. The only difference between us is in understanding. You think you have lost it. I think I have got it. When you, too, develop the right understanding, you will realize that everything is inside you and that you can perceive everything within yourself. There was a great Sufi saint named Kabir Sahib, who was a devotee of Rama. He said, "Inside me there is Kashi, Prayag, the holy rivers, Mecca with its great mosque, and all other places of worship. When everything is inside me, why should I perform any external worship?" There is no greater deity than the Self. Increase and enhance this awareness. Do not try to teach or to learn phony practices that waste people's time and life and understanding. Do not try to learn how to fly, because you are not a bird. Do not try to learn how to sit on water, because you are not a fish. Pursue the Self, because you *are* the Self. Take care of your Self. Learn how to become ecstatic within yourself. Ecstasy is inside, not outside. The one you are looking for, the one you want to attain, is you.

Therefore, the *Kularnava Tantra* says that the best practice is to become immersed within yourself. You are not different from God, nor is God different from you. You are not far away from God, nor is God far away from you. If you think you are far away from God, that is due to the delusion of your own mind. If you give the delusion of your mind to the psychologists, then whatever is left will be the Self.

Everything Is His Own Glory

When a person follows the path of the Siddhas, he attains the bliss of Consciousness within himself. Then he sees the same bliss within

196 THE NATURAL STATE

everything; when he looks at other people and at the different objects
of the world, he enjoys the same ecstasy. One of the *sutras* of the
Shiva Sutras is *Lokanandah samadhi sukham* — "The bliss of the world
is the ecstasy of *samadhi*." This means that to entertain the awareness
of equality and to see God within everyone is to experience the
bliss of *samadhi*. A Siddha sees everyone as not different from himself.
That is why he sees no high or low. That is why he accepts everyone
and discards no one. For a Siddha, Shiva is the action, Shiva is the
instrument of action, and Shiva is all the senses. This is the way the
Siddhas do their *sadhana*; this is why they see no one as different
from themselves. Siddha Yoga teaches one to do the *sadhana* of
this awareness and, in this way, to become Shiva and to understand
that nothing is different from the Self.

Parashiva says, "Everything is the play of universal Consciousness."
When this is the case, how can you say that one thing is good and
something else bad? What can you accept or reject? Where is Shiva
not? In what does Shiva not exist? Jnaneshwar Maharaj said, "O
Lord of the Self, when You hide Yourself, You appear as this world,
but when You reveal Yourself, everything is seen as Consciousness,
as the Self." To have this awareness that everything is the embodiment
of the Self is the goal of Siddha Yoga.

Therefore, a person should become established in that knowledge,
in the awareness that everything is his own glory. Kabir Sahib called
this state *sahaja samadhi*, the natural state of *samadhi*. This is not
the *samadhi* you attain by isolating yourself in a room or a cave, by
shutting your eyes or stopping your breath or plugging your nostrils.
This is the natural state of *samadhi*, and it is great. It is attained
only by a person whose inner Shakti has been awakened and
unfolded by the grace of the Guru. Through the workings of the
inner Shakti, the mind which has been wandering here and there
becomes quiet in the inner Self. It merges in the Self, and then the
trouble of the mind ceases. As the mind becomes one-pointed, the
individual soul becomes established in the *sahasrara*, the topmost
spiritual center. He attains the state of being a witness, the state of
witness-consciousness. Then he sees that same Consciousness
everywhere.

This is the natural state of *samadhi* — to experience equality
everywhere and in everything, to see the same thing equally in all

trees, in all creepers, in all gods, in all beings, and in all creatures and to become established in this natural state spontaneously. Kabir Sahib said, "When my Guru made me realize that space, when my Guru made me realize that Consciousness, I began to revel in the following state: Wherever I walked, it was my pilgrimage; it was my way to get to God. Whatever work I did was service to God. When I slept, that was the way I prostrated before Him. Whatever I said and whatever I heard was the mantra. My eating, my drinking, my bathing were all worship of God."

No matter what you are doing, it is the Self, the Lord, who is experiencing everything. One of the verses in the hymn *Mental Worship of Shiva* says, "O Lord, You are the Self. Your divine power, Your Shakti, is my understanding. Your companions exist as my five *pranas*. Whatever I do, whether I eat, whether I drink, whether I look, whatever I do to entertain myself is my worship of You."

Kabir Sahib also said, "When I eat, when I drink, I worship Him. O *sadhus*, this is the natural state of *samadhi*. My own house and the bare ground appear the same to me. I discarded the notion of duality, and when duality was erased, the natural state of *samadhi* came to me on its own. Now, I don't have to close my eyes. I don't have to plug my ears. I don't have to give any trouble to the body. I don't have to close my eyes to meditate, because with my eyes open I can see the beautiful Self. I have gotten into this natural state of *samadhi*. Inside, I continually hear the divine sounds of So'ham, So'ham. As my mind became immersed in that sound, the filth of the mind left me." The filth of the mind is nothing but the notion of duality. "Now I hear this sound all the time, ceaselessly — when I stand up, when I sit down, when I go, when I come. The constant flow of this sound always exists and it is unbroken." Kabir Sahib said, "This is the state which is beyond the mind. Though I have sung it, though I have revealed it to you, it is the inner secret."

That supreme state exists right inside of you. It is one with you. It is not that God gave this state only to Kabir. Kabir was a person like the rest of us — he wasn't a special cousin-brother of God. The same state is inside you. It is the state you attain when you become established in the awareness of Consciousness; it is beyond both joy and grief. A wise person knows that joy is not really joy, and grief is not really grief. These are simply the things you experience in certain states. If something goes in your favor, you experience happiness. If something is against you, you experience unhappiness. However, that same thing may be in someone else's favor, and that person will experience happiness. So Kabir said, "The supreme state, the abode of God, is beyond pain and pleasure. O *sadhu*, I have entered the natural state of *samadhi*, which is great."

State of a Saint

Q: What is the spiritual state of a saint?

SM: A saint's state is not something that you can talk about. You have to become a saint and experience it. There was a great woman saint, Yogini Rabi'a, who lived in Basra. She wrote many things that people still read today. She used to go to Kaaba every day to offer her prayers. However, once she became ill for two days and because of her power, Kaaba itself—that stone itself—went to her. Someone asked her this question: "Can you explain the state of those beings who are absorbed and immersed in the state of God, in the love of God?" Rabi'a said, "If I try to explain that, then I will be in the same situation as a person in the waking state who tries to explain the state of a person who is sleeping. To know the experiences of the sleeping state, you will have to go deep into the sleeping state."

A saint attains the state in which he becomes one with God. Whatever a person pursues, whomever he worships, he imbibes those qualities. Once a good woman came to meet me. She was a householder and had children. She said, "I pray to God all the time, and when I pray I become one with Jesus. However, when I become immersed in him, I begin to feel a lot of pain in my palms, and I cannot bear that pain." So to whomever you pray, whomever you worship, you attain the state of that being. I felt very happy when I listened to her. I told her not to worry and not to be afraid, that her palms might give her pain for awhile, but that it was all right. I said, "Right now, you are meditating on his body. Try to enter into his inner Self, and then you will not feel this physical pain, because once you reach that state, there is no pain."

A miserable person is in the state of pain. A happy person is in the state of happiness. A deluded person is in the state of delusion.

In the same way, there is another state, a greater state, in which
you become absorbed in God. The state of a saint is the state of
God-consciousness. As he meditates continuously, his inner energy
is unfolded and then he reaches the space of God. Once he becomes
established in that space, he attains the state of God. Then, even
though he has this human body, even though he still appears to be
a human being outwardly, inwardly he lives as Consciousness. He
becomes immersed in God, he becomes anchored in God, and he
always lives in that awareness. He never has this egotistical feeling.
He always is aware that he is That. If a person is diseased, his
entire being, his breath and his blood, all contain the germs of his
disease. In the same way, the nectar of love, the nectar of the ecstasy
of God, pervades every pore and hair of the body of a saint.

If you ask me to describe the nature of that state as it is, the
only way that I can describe it is by being silent. In that state, there
are no thoughts. In that state, there are no variations. That state is
nothing but love and peace. This is how the state of a saint is. So
you should become a saint.

The State of My Own Understanding

Q: Please explain the state that you are in.

SM: I live in the state of my own understanding. Everybody exists
in the state of his understanding, and whatever state of understanding
he lives in, so he becomes. Most of the time you live in the thoughts
of your mind, and according to those thoughts, you experience pain
or pleasure, enmity, jealousy, pride, or other conditions. However,
I do not attach importance to any thought that arises in my mind,
nor do I identify myself with any of them. I just witness their coming
and going. If I have good thoughts, I do not become happy. If I
have bad thoughts, I do not become unhappy. Most of the time,
you feel "I am this body." However, I feel that I am different from
this body. A great Sufi saint said, "The mind undergoes trouble
the moment you have the awareness 'I am this body.'" Instead of
identifying with this body, I turn within. If I go beyond the conscious
mind, the subconscious mind, and the intellect, then I realize that I
am nothing but the effulgent light of the Self, and I begin to swim
in the ocean of that brilliance.

Whether you are a person of knowledge or a dull person, whether you are enlightened or not, your way of living is the same. However, there is a difference in your understanding. Therefore, a great saint said, "Close the door of your individuality, your ego. Do not let your ego leak out. Once you close the door of your ego, what is left? Nothing but *sat, chit,* and *ananda*—existence absolute, consciousness absolute, and bliss absolute." Mostly, you are afraid to lose the seed of your ego. But you should think of it in this way: When you sow a mustard seed, it seemingly loses itself in the earth. However, after awhile, it sprouts and grows into a plant. So a great Sufi saint said, "If you want to attain the Truth, if you want to become an ideal being, if you want to become divine, then give up your ego. Lose your individuality completely. Who said you cannot attain God?" A person who gives up his petty ego, who loses his ego in meditation on the Self, attains everything. He can create a new world within himself.

Therefore, I always live in this awareness: I am not this body; I am Consciousness. I lose myself in this awareness most of the time. Sometimes I may come out of it, but I know how to return to it. Although I live in this body, I am separate from this body. Although I live with my understanding, I am different from my understanding. I live right in the junction point between pain and pleasure. For this reason, I am extremely happy. I continually remember Him, and nothing else.

Once someone asked Rabi'a, "O Rabi'a, do you ever experience pain or pleasure?" She said, "Yes. Whenever I forget my own Self."

Growing Teeth

Q: If you are in the God-realized state, why can't you grow teeth?

SM: I have teeth—they are sitting inside my room. What makes you think a God-realized being should be a dentist or a dental technician? Your next question might be, "If you are a God-realized being, why do you need somebody to give you a shave? Why don't you just dematerialize your beard?" Then you may ask, "If you are a God-realized being, why should you have your clothes laundered by somebody else? Why can't you have them washed automatically

by your powers?" You don't know what God-realization means. You
have kindergarten ideas. An ordinary dental technician can make
dentures. What's the use of using spiritual power to make teeth?
What's the point of spending it for that trivial end? Besides, the
body has its own physical limitations, and if a person happens to
lose his teeth, why should he want them back again? Why can't he
accept it? I can talk and explain things to you and sing without
teeth, and if I were to use my dentures, I would be speaking, talking, and singing in the same way.

It's wrong to think that God is there to satisfy your trivial
needs—that if you have lost your teeth, He should supply you with
new ones, and if you have lost your nails, He should supply you
with new ones, and if you have caught a chill and have a bad cough
or a sore throat, He should heal or cure that. Anyone who is intelligent and wise will use spiritual power only for helping people to
realize God. That spiritual power has been obtained as a result of
God-realization, and it should be used only for that.

This reminds me of a story. King Akbar was a great king of
India. Once he went hunting, and as he was chasing his prey he
went farther and farther and farther into the forest. The sun was
pouring down heat, and Akbar started feeling tired and also very
hungry. At last he came upon a shepherd, whose name was Ramja.
Akbar said to him, "Can you give me something to eat?" Ramja was
a very simple man, and he had only the plainest fare, but he mixed
up whatever he had into a kind of gruel and served it to the king in
a large pot. The king had never tasted such a thing before in his
life, but since he was very hungry he enjoyed it very much. There is
a saying in our country: "If you are hungry, you don't need delicacies. And if you are sleepy, you don't need a soft bed." Akbar
enjoyed the gruel thoroughly. He was very pleased, and said to
Ramja, "I'm so grateful to you for your welcome, and you served me
with great courtesy. If you ever come to my capital, come straight to
me. Whatever you ask of me I'll give to you." Then he left a letter
of authority with Ramja. After a while there was a marriage in
Ramja's family, and he went to the capital. He remembered that
the king had given him a letter of authority, so he went to the
palace. Akbar welcomed Ramja warmly and served him royal delicacies. The next morning he said to Ramja, "Ramja, you helped
me so much. You are a poor subject of mine; ask me for any boon,

and I promise that I'll grant it to you." Ramja lived in the country
and he was addicted to chewing tobacco. In India, before people
chew tobacco, they rub slake lime into the tobacco. Ramja didn't
have any slake lime, so he said to the king, "Your majesty, could
you kindly get me one kilo of slake lime?" Ramja could have asked
for a big estate from the king, but all that he asked for was slake
lime.

So if a God-realized being were to start materializing glasses and
dentures or dematerializing illnesses, then he would be just like
Ramja. Instead of asking for a spiritual kingdom from God, he would
be asking for slake lime.

No Seeing

Q: If I were in *samadhi*, would I experience being God myself, or
would I just witness God? In other words, would I have an experience or would I be the experience?

SM: This is a question you should answer after doing *sadhana*; it's
not for asking. Meditate a bit and see what God is like—whether
He is the witness or whether He pervades everything. When you
are absorbed in God, there is no seeing and no being seen. One
man who experienced this wrote:

> The lila of Krishna, the dear enchanter, the sweet lover,
> is just this:
> We lost ourselves completely;
> we knew not who we were.

A Good Time

Q: What do you do to have a good time?

SM: The moment I experience a divine presence around me, the
presence of the great One, immediately I have a good time. I just
become so happy. Whenever my mind, my subconscious mind, and
my intellect turn inward, the moment I have a glimpse of That, joy
shimmers inside. I consider that to be a good time. I don't believe

that happiness exists outside, because I have seen that nobody can find happiness in wealth. I have seen many wealthy people who are not happy, many radio and television interviewers who are not happy, many architects who are not happy, many scientists who are not happy. Nobody is happy; everybody is unhappy. Only the Self is filled with happiness. For this reason, I remain immersed in God. I am happy all the time.

If God Is Everywhere

Q: If God is everywhere and in everything, why can't we see Him?

SM: We can't see Him because we don't try to find out what He looks like. I'll give you an example. When you get sick, can you see the origin of your sickness? Only a doctor can. If you were a doctor, you too could see where it came from. First you have to have the eye to see it. God is everywhere, there's no doubt about that, but you have to have the right eye to see Him. Look at the air. It blows everywhere, but you can't see it. You can only feel it when it touches you. Your question implies that God can be seen. Sit quietly for a while and meditate on the Self. You'll be able to see Him. In what form would you like to see God? He has taken the form of bread in this piece of bread—don't try to see Him as stone in bread. In fruit you should see God as fruit, in a tree you should see God as a tree, and in yourself you should see Him as yourself. Who says that God cannot be seen? Don't try to see Him as different from the way He has manifested Himself. Try to see Him as He is. Once someone went to a *rishi* with a sheet and said, "Why can't I see cotton in this sheet?" The *rishi* said, "Cotton became this sheet. Why can't you see it as it is, as cotton? What's the point of tearing the sheet into pieces and separating out the threads? Why can't you see the sheet as cotton?" Go and sit for a while. I'm very pleased with your question.

Individualists

Q: Once a person has attained God-realization and no longer has to exist with the physical body, does he continue to keep some individual aspect to serve God? Does he continue to be God's servant eternally, or does he actually merge with the Absolute and become God?

SM: Once a person's individuality has merged with God, then all feeling of separateness is finished. What remains is the feeling of Godhood. If a river is flowing and meets with the ocean, then it merges into the ocean and the individual existence of the river is finished. However, the ocean still exists. What happens in the state of realization is that a person's individuality merges into God. Then he attains cosmic awareness. After that, he serves other people. Many people have the feeling that once a person attains God-realization he becomes useless. But has God retired? So far He has not retired. He continues to function. For this reason, a person who has attained God will continue to serve other people. His goal will be to make others attain God.

The Inner Lights

Q: Did all realized beings have the same vision of the different worlds and colored lights and the same experience of the blue pearl, or do they differ for different people?

SM: The inner kingdom of the Self is the same for everybody. Inside, there are different colored lights. They are brilliant and they are all the same for everybody. If you meditate systematically, then certainly you will see them. The inner Self contains infinite light. It is only because its light exists that there is radiance in a human being, that you feel interest in others.

The experiences of all realized beings are the same. However, each of them describes his own experiences in his own way. Jagadguru Shankaracharya said, "The Shaivities call Him Shiva. The Vedantins call Him Brahman. People who follow the path of devotion see Him as the object of devotion. People who follow rituals believe that He is the giver of the fruits of their rituals. So everybody describes the same One in many different ways. Nonetheless, He is only one throughout all the three worlds, and it is He who manipulates everything." Every person experiences the same state, the same God.

God is not aware of different directions. For Him there is no difference between east, west, south, and north. He is all-pervasive. All countries, all languages, all forms, all names, all colors, all actions, and all religions belong to Him. He dwells within all equally. So everybody has the same experience of Him.

Bliss and Pain

Q: When you were sick, did you experience physical pain; if so, did physical pain affect your inner bliss? Can bliss and pain exist at the same time in one person?

SM: Once Hassan asked Rabi'a, "Rabi'a, do you ever remember me?" She said, "Yes, Hassan, whenever I forget God, I remember you. But if I am absorbed in remembrance of God, then I never remember you." In the same way, when I was ill, if I looked at my body, I began to feel that I was sick, but when I was absorbed in my inner bliss, I did not know that I was sick. The pain of the physical body doesn't reach the subtler bodies. It isn't possible to laugh and cry at the same time. In the same way, how can it be possible to experience bliss and pain at the same time? Physical pain does not affect the inner bliss, it affects only the physical body. Physical pain doesn't even reach you when you are sleeping. So a sadhu always lives beyond this state of body-consciousness. A sadhu's state is very well described as a state where the heat of the sun cannot reach, where the coolness of the moon cannot reach, and where even pain cannot enter. When a person is always established in supreme bliss, even death cannot reach him. After you attain this state, it never leaves you. This is the place where yogis abide, and this is the body of a yogi.

God Within Everybody

Q: How do you see God?

SM: I see God in all of you. There is no other way to see God. The Lord Himself said to Arjuna, "O Arjuna, understand that only he has the vision to see Me who becomes aware that the creation, sustenance, and dissolution of this entire universe take place within Me." So I see God within everybody. I do not see God as separate from anyone. If God is not within me, if God is not before me, if God is not behind me, if God is not on all sides, if God is not within the people who surround me, then I am not interested in Him. Why should I bother to see some God who stays far away? Therefore, first I perceive God within my Self, and then I see God within everybody with the awareness that just as He exists within me He exists within all. Even on the gallows, Mansur Mastana had this awareness. He said, "In the temple, people worship an idol. In the mosque, there is no idol, only a void. People go to these places to find God. However, the heart is the true temple, the true mosque of God, and God's radiance exists within." For this reason, I welcome everybody with respect every day. You will know That within your Self. You will receive messages from within, and you will see God within your Self. So see God in this way.

From My Viewpoint, You Are the Truth

Q: We are reminded again and again that life is impermanent. I would like to know what people should do when you eventually leave your body?

SM: Life is not completely impermanent; we can make it permanent. Life itself is beautiful; it is so bewitching. It can be anything that we want it to be. God gave birth to this creation from His own being, and it is not different from Him. God is very disciplined, very regular. He makes every second come at the right time. Why aren't we like that? We should think about this very carefully.

Q: When a person dies, the impermanent parts of his being must disappear, leaving something permanent. What is it that remains after physical death?

SM: That is the Truth, the Self, God. That is Consciousness or Shakti, energy. Because of That we are able to perform all actions. The supreme Truth never changes; it always remains the same. It is not tainted by impurity or by purity or by anything else. Due to that Consciousness we are able to perform actions. We always say, "I, I,

I," but we are not aware of the true nature of that "I." When we say "I," do we mean the parts of this body? The *prana* helps this body to function, but when we say "I" do we mean the *prana*? The Self of the universe, God, exists inside this body and makes the universe work. Are we aware which "I" is "I"?

Q: So that "I" is not really a personal being. That "I" is not Baba Muktananda.

SM: That "I" is the supreme Truth. That "I" is Consciousness, and it has become everything. From this "I" many worlds arise and subside. From one seed comes a tree; from one tree come many seeds; from these seeds come many trees. Even before the trees exist, the seed is there. The seed of this world is the "I," supreme Truth, Consciousness, and it is the same for everybody. It belongs equally to all. That Consciousness exists within itself, and in the same measure it exists in us and in everyone—in you, in me, in Nityananda my Guru, in Buddha, in Mohammed, in Moses, in Jesus.

Q: So when this form of Muktananda passes away, that same supreme "I" will remain exactly as it is now?

SM: Yes, it will remain the same. Even if the body leaves, That does not leave. The body comes and goes, but That always remains. I can explain this to you in simple words. Just as the inner space of this room remains whether or not the walls are standing, so regardless of the body's impermanence, That is permanent. Some people call it God. Whether you call it God or Rama or Allah, that Truth remains the same.

Q: But there seems to be a special manifestation, for instance, through Baba. The supreme "I" is not as clearly manifest through other people. What is that particular stream of manifestation that we call Baba Muktananda?

SM: The inner Truth that exists inside me also exists inside you and everybody else. There isn't the slightest difference. The only difference is that I have turned within and perceived it. I have made That reveal itself to me. You don't turn within and see it because you always want to be focused outside. If you would also turn within, then the same stream that flows out of my body would flow out of yours. Truly speaking, in God's creation there is no disparity. There is only equality. In one factory the same objects are manufactured. They are all identical. Similarly, everything is the same in the Lord's factory.

Q: Still, there appears to be some difference, because people find their spiritual consciousness being awakened in the presence of Baba but not in the presence of others—even other spiritual teachers.

SM: There may be such a difference now, but if everybody were to become like me, then the difference would vanish.

Q: What would be left?

SM: Only the supreme Truth.

Q: Still manifesting as the world or formless?

SM: Even in the form of the world the Truth exists. The world is not different from the Truth. Water becomes ice, and ice becomes water again. In the same way, the world comes out of the supreme Truth. That Truth exists in the world, and the world belongs to it. Just as hair and nails come from our body, the world comes out of the supreme Truth. For this reason, Kashmir Shaivism says, "The world is the play of Consciousness." The first aphorism of the *Shiva Sutras* is, "The Self is Consciousness." The world is Consciousness.

Q: Baba, you have opened a door into pure Consciousness for those who love you. Will that door stay open through you for the next one hundred or two hundred years?

SM: It will always remain open, because this lineage will never be broken. Baba Nityananda, my Guru, gave me his work to do. Similarly, when I leave this world, I will have to make somebody else responsible for the work. When one president leaves, another comes. When that one leaves, a third one comes.

Q: It seems that people who have been close to you have received your grace to the point where they can transmit it to some extent to other people. I wanted to say that we are very grateful that these people are working in this country.

SM: Yes, many people are working in the same line. The Shakti is working in all of them. Many will also do this work in the future. This mission will continue to increase. Many will do the work.

Q: In your autobiography, *Play of Consciousness*, we read about your marvelous experiences in which you feel that your true being is permeating everything on all planes. I assume that some day, when this form of Baba Muktananda disappears, your special presence will always be felt on all planes of being.

SM: Yes, that will remain in all planes, continuing to do the work. My Baba, my Guru, is still working. Even if you put his photo somewhere, people feel something from it. People should not feel that this is strange. What place exists without Consciousness? So that Consciousness exists in the photo, too.

Q: When you say your Guru, Baba Nityananda, do you mean anything other than the supreme "I"? Is there something particular about him?

SM: The supreme Truth is Nityananda. In Nityananda, the supreme Truth existed, and the same supreme Truth became Nityananda.

Q: Can we ask the same question about Jesus and Rama and other great beings? Are they really nothing more than the supreme Truth, or are there different lineages extending from these different beings?

SM: The Self is the same in all of them. However, their particular mission may have been different. Take, for example, Krishna. People who lived in his time said that he was the incarnation of the supreme Truth. He was never defeated by wicked people. A great being, an incarnation of the supreme Truth, is one who is never defeated by anybody, who never falls. However, from the viewpoint of the Self, everyone is the same.

Q: You spoke about the fact that different teachers could have different missions. Can you say something about what your mission is in this life?

SM: My mission is not any particular religion. It is a spiritual revolution. My teaching is: Look within. Understand your own Self.

Perceive your own Self. Attain your own Self. I teach that to learn this, you don't have to depend on external things. I don't say that somebody lives up above and that one day he will come down to help you. I don't deny the existence of God above, but I say that He is inside you, too, in the same measure. So look within and attain Him right inside yourself. I do not give any importance to class or caste or particular religions or anything of that kind. It does not matter whether you are black or white or yellow or red. All colors and all classes have come from God. I do not like to make any distinctions. My purpose is to say, "The supreme Truth exists inside everybody, so look within, perceive That, and attain That."

Q: Just by looking within no one will achieve anything if they don't have your grace.

SM: It is true that you need grace also. When I tell you, "Look within, enter inside," grace follows with those words.

Q: It's not like the ordinary words "Look within." Somehow when Baba says to look within it contains the actual Shakti, the energy that makes it possible.

SM: You are absolutely right. Both the grace and Shakti follow those words. The Shakti, the energy of the Self, is so great.

Q: There may be thousands of people listening to this program, Baba. Please tell them to look within and transmit that Shakti right now.

SM: Not only thousands—I want to tell the entire world. Give up your notions of different castes, different classes, different sects, different religions. Stop moving on the outside. Enter within, and see what you perceive inside. The reason you perceive differences between one society and another, between one caste and another, between one country and another is because you are only looking outside. If you turn within and attain the inner Self, then you will see the same inner Self in all countries, in all individuals, and in all places. You will see and experience the same divine bliss everywhere. If everyone were to look within and perceive the inner Self, weapons would become unnecessary. Nations wouldn't have to have hatred and hostility toward one another or bomb one another and plot each other's destruction. God has created this world for His own pleasure. He has created wealth for His own joy. We use this wealth not for our own good, for our own pleasure, but to make poisonous ammunitions.

Q: Even the ignorance of human beings, even their tendency to look outside, must also be a part of God's play.

SM: It is the result of forgetting God.

Q: But if everything is the play of Consciousness, how can one forget? How can Consciousness forget itself?

SM: It's not that Consciousness has forgotten itself. We ourselves have kept Consciousness other than ourselves. A king who is sleeping dreams that he has become a beggar, and he weeps and wails; however, when the king wakes up, he laughs at himself because he thought that he had become a beggar. We are in the same predicament.

Q: But the king has certain *samskaras* or tendencies, and that's why he would have the dream of being a beggar. But there are no tendencies or *samskaras* in pure Consciousness, so how can it have this dream of being limited persons?

SM: There is no limitation in Consciousness. It is our own *samskaras* from the past which make us feel that we are contracted. Due to these *samskaras* we become contracted. Once we have right understanding, we again expand. Therefore, a person should expand himself.

Q: Doesn't some of the highest Vedantic teaching imply that there is ultimately no expansion or contraction?

SM: It is very true. Once you attain that ultimate understanding, then there is nothing. Then you will know that everything is the expansion or the pervasion of Consciousness. Therefore, Shaivism says, "The world is the sport of Consciousness."

Q: So when you, Baba, look at the seekers of Truth who come here and see them expanding and contracting in their own eyes, you really ultimately don't see anything except the play of Consciousness — no expansion and no contraction?

SM: From my point of view, they are not contracted, but they think they are contracted. When you take ornaments to the goldsmith, he looks only at the gold; he does not look at the ornaments in their different shapes and sizes. However, if the customer goes there, he looks at the outward forms. He does not look only at the gold.

Q: Baba, thank you for sharing our limited dreams and nightmares with us even though you remain beyond the dream state.

SM: It is not that I share your dreams. From your viewpoint you are dreaming, but from my viewpoint you are the Truth. You watch your own dream, but I don't watch your dreams; I see you as my own Self.

Q: From Baba's point of view there really are no dreams? There are no limitations? There are no individuals apart from pure Consciousness?

SM: Yes, there is only the play of Consciousness—only the drama, only the dance of Consciousness. When there is an ordinary drama on the stage, there is a producer. How does he look at the drama? Isn't it a mere play for him?

Q: You always mention the play of Consciousness and the dance of Consciousness. Why does it play? Why doesn't it remain entirely still?

SM: Even while it is playing, its stillness is not disturbed. In the ocean so many waves leap up and down, up and down. Although that happens, the ocean's profundity is not disturbed.

Q: So Shakti is the playful aspect and Shiva is the absolutely still aspect?

SM: Yes, supreme Shiva always remains supremely serene, quiet, and still. The Shakti that vibrates from Him does all the playing.

Q: Does the union of Shiva and Shakti mean that the play and the stillness exist exactly at the same time and are actually synonymous?

SM: Even when the play takes place, the stillness is not disturbed. For example, now I am moving my hands, making gestures, but that inner stillness is not disturbed. In the same way, even while the play goes on, the total stillness of the supreme Truth is not disturbed. It is a matter of understanding.

Q: Are some people more drawn to the supreme stillness and others drawn to the play?

SM: Most people are drawn to the play. The reason for this is that they do not have knowledge of the Truth.

Q: Baba, please bless us that we can be drawn to the stillness and grant us "*shivapat*" as well as *shaktipat*.

SM: From all your questions I understand and believe that you do have the understanding of Shiva to a certain extent.

Q: Please bless us that it may increase and deepen.

SM: It will keep increasing and increasing and increasing. It will keep increasing to that state of Shiva. Once you reach that state, it will rest. Even if people were to hear this much, it would be enough for them. I give this message to everybody, not to a particular society or class. My message is: Meditate on your own Self, understand your own Self, attain your own Self. The supreme Truth dwells within you as you. In infinite forms He pervades everywhere; however, He is one. However we categorize Him, there is no division in Him. We should stop categorizing Him and should see Him as one. Whatever there is, it is all Him.

GLOSSARY

Arati: The waving of lights or incense before a saint or deity as an act of worship.

Auliya: A saint or great being.

Arjuna: A famous warrior and one of the heroes of the *Mahabharata* epic. It was to Arjuna that Krishna imparted the teaching of the *Bhagavad Gita*.

Ashram: A residential community where spiritual discipline is practiced; the abode of a saint or holy man.

Aurobindo: A twentieth-century yogi and scholar who wrote extensively on issues of social reform as well as on spirituality.

Bhagavad Gita: The most popular Hindu scripture; a portion of the *Mahabharata* in which Lord Krishna instructs Arjuna about the path of liberation.

Bhakti Sutras: The classic scripture of the path of devotion; attributed to the sage Narada.

Bharadwaja: A sage of Puranic fame who devoted his life to the constant study of the Vedas.

Bhartrihari: A king who renounced his kingdom in order to become a yogi; author of many spiritual poems.

Bhavantha Ramayana: Eknath Maharaj's sixteenth-century rendition of Valmiki's *Ramayana*, composed in the Marathi language.

Bhikshu: A mendicant, monk, or *sannyasi*.

Brahmananda: A great poet and yogi of the nineteenth century who wrote *Ishwara Darshan* ("the vision of God").

Chandogya Upanishad: A portion of the teachings of the ancient sages on the essential nature of absolute Reality.

Chapati: Unleavened Indian bread that looks like a pancake.

Consciousness: The intelligent, supremely autonomous energy that manifests, pervades, and supports everything in the cosmos.

Ego: Limited "I"-awareness, which identifies with limiting attributes such as the mind or the body.

Eklavya: A tribal boy who mastered the art of archery by worshipping and practicing before an image of his Guru, Dronacharya. Cited as an example of an ideal disciple; from the *Mahabharata*.

Eknath Maharaj (1528-1609): A householder poet-saint of Maharashtra renowned for his scriptural commentaries and spiritual poetry.

Ganeshpuri: An ancient sacred place in the state of Maharashtra in India where Swami Muktananda's Guru, Bhagawan Nityananda, settled and where Gurudev Siddha Peeth is located.

Ganga (Ganges): The most sacred river in India, which flows from the Himalayas through North India. It is believed that whoever bathes in the Ganges is purified of all sins.

Ghee: Clarified butter used in Indian cooking and worship.

Guru: A spiritual master who has attained oneness with God and who initiates others into the spiritual path and guides them to liberation.

Gurudev Siddha Peeth: The name given by Swami Muktananda to his ashram in Ganeshpuri.

Hasan of Basra (642-748): One of the early Sufi saints; a great orator noted for his piety.

Hasrat Mussa: A Muslim prophet.

Jain: A member of a religious system originating in India in the sixth century BC that stressed strict asceticism and solicitude for all life.

Janaka: A saintly king of Mithila in ancient India; father of Sita, Lord Rama's consort.

Japa: Repetition of the mantra.

Jnaneshwari: A brilliant commentary on the *Bhagavad Gita* written by Jnaneshwar Maharaj in the thirteenth century.

Jnaneshwar Maharaj (1275-1296): A highly revered poet-saint of Maharashtra whose commentary on the *Bhagavad Gita*—*Jnaneshwari*—is acknowledged as one of the world's most important spiritual works.

Kabir (1440-1518): A renowned Indian poet-saint who was a weaver in Benares. His followers were both Hindus and Muslims, and his influence was a powerful force in overcoming religious factionalism.

Kali (lit. "the black one"): A form of the universal mother, or Shakti. She is a fierce aspect of Shakti, represented as a young woman naked to the waist, wearing a necklace of skulls and standing on a prone male figure.

Kalyan Swami: A disciple of Samartha Ramdas.

Kapilamuni: A sage and yogi of ancient India; founder of the Sankhya system of philosophy.

Karma: Physical, mental or verbal action or the results of such action.

Kashmir Shaivism: A nondual philosophy that recognizes the entire universe as a manifestation of divine conscious energy.

King Akbar: A sixteenth century Mogul emperor of India noted for his policy of religious tolerance.

King Shivaji: A wise and noble king who ruled Maharashtra during the seventeenth century and was a disciple of Samartha Ramdas.

Krishna: Eighth incarnation of Vishnu, whose life story is described in the *Shrimad Bhagavatam* and the *Mahabharata* and whose teachings are contained in the *Bhagavad Gita*.

Kriya (lit. "movement"): A yogic movement or process taking place after the awakening of Kundalini.

Kularnava Tantra: Treatise on yoga; a basic work of the Kaula school of North Indian tantrism.

Lila: Divine play. Creation is often explained in Hinduism as the *lila*, or divine play, of God.

Lokmanya Tilak: A nineteenth-century Indian political leader who worked ceaselessly for independence from British rule.

Lukman: A great physician and Muslim saint.

Mahabharata: An Indian epic composed by the sage Vyasa delineating the struggles of two families over a kingdom. The rich and varied story of the epic contains the definitive teaching on right action *(dharma)* according to Indian thought.

Maharashtra: A state in West India in which Gurudev Siddha Peeth is located. It has been the home of many great saints.

Mahasamadhi (lit. "the great *samadhi*"): The conscious death of a yogi.

Mahatma (lit. "great soul"): A Hindu title of respect for a man renowned for spirituality.

Mansur Mastana (Mansur Al-Hullaj) (858-913): An ecstatic Sufi saint who was accused of heresy and was hanged for proclaiming his identity with God.

Mantra: A sacred word or sound invested with the power to transform and protect one who repeats it.

Maya: The power which veils the real nature of the Self so that the universe is seen as separate from the Self and the individual is seen as separate from God.

Mira(bai) (1433-1468): A Rajasthani queen and poet-saint famous for her beautiful poems of devotion to Lord Krishna.

Namdev: A thirteenth-century poet-saint of Maharashtra; a tailor by trade who was a contemporary of Jnaneshwar and disciple of Visoba Khechara.

Narada: A famous sage of the Puranas who was a noted musician and author of the *Bhakti Sutras*.

Nipat Niranjan: A poet-saint and disciple of Bhartrihari.

Nityananda (?-1961) (lit. "eternal bliss"): Famous twentieth-century saint and Guru of Swami Muktananda.

Pakoras: Vegetables deep-fried in a batter.

Patanjali Yoga Sutras: The classical exposition of the eightfold path of yoga written in the second century by Patanjali; the authoritative text on *raja* yoga.

Prakasha: Light; the aspect of consciousness that illumines.

Prana: The vital force of the body and universe which sustains life.

Pranayama: Control of *prana*; breathing exercise.

Prasad: (1 A blessed or divine gift. (2 Food that has been blessed by being offered to God.

Pratyabhijnahridayam (lit. "the heart of the doctrine of recognition"): A text of twenty sutras on Kashmir Shaivism with commentaries by Kshemaraja.

Puja: Worship.

Puranas: Mythological and historical stories; part of the Hindu scriptures.

Puri: An Indian form of deep-fried bread.

Purno'ham: Literally, "the perfect I."

Rabi'a(717-801): Great Sufi saint and yogini who lived in Basra.

Rajas: Activity, passion; one of the three basic qualities of nature which determine the inherent characteristics of all created things.

Rama: An incarnation of God; the central character in the Indian epic, the *Ramayana*; the supreme Lord who pervades all beings and all things.

Ramayana (lit. "history of Rama"): The oldest of the Sanskrit epic poems written by the sage Valmiki. It celebrates the life and exploits of Rama, the seventh incarnation of Vishnu.

Ram Tirth (1873-1906): Renowned mathematician, philosopher, poet, and saint who lectured on Vedanta in India, Japan, and America.

Rishi: A seer of Truth; the term is applied to the sages to whom the Vedas and other scriptures were revealed.

Sadguru: A true Guru; divine master. See also: Guru.

Sadhana: The practice of spiritual discipline.

Sadhu: A holy being, monk, or ascetic.

Sahaja samadhi: The spontaneous state of *samadhi* which remains continuous and unbroken throughout the waking, dream, and deep sleep states.

Saint Augustine (354-430): A famous Christian theologian, a bishop, and a doctor of the early Latin church.

Samadhi: State of meditative union with the Absolute.

Samartha Ramdas: A seventeenth century saint who was the Guru of King Shivaji and the spiritual inspiration behind the Maratha uprising against Mogul rule.

Samskara: Impression of past action or thought lingering in the subconscious.

Sannyasa: Initiation into monkhood in the Indian tradition.

Saraswati Order: An order of monks founded by Shankaracharya in the eighth century to teach the philosophy of absolute nondualism.

Satsang: A meeting of devotees to hear spiritual teaching, chant, or sit in the presence of the Guru; the company of saints and devotees.

Seera: An Indian pudding made of wheat, *ghee*, and sugar.

Seva (guruseva): Service to the Guru.

Shaivism: See: Kashmir Shaivism.

Shakti (Chiti, Chiti Kundalini, Kundalini, Kundalini Shakti): The divine energy which manifests, maintains, and dissolves the universe; consort of Shiva.

Shaktipat: (1 Transmission of spiritual power (Shakti) from the Guru to the disciple. (2 Spiritual awakening by grace.

Shankaracharya (780-820): One of the major philosopher-saints of the Indian tradition, who expounded the philosophy of absolute non-dualism (Advaita).

Sheikh Nasrudin: A folklore figure originating in Turkey during the Middle Ages, used by spiritual teachers to illustrate the antics characteristic of the human mind.

Sheikh Sadi (1184-1291): Renowned Sufi scholar and author of *The Gulistan*, a collection of allegorical tales.

Shems of Tabriez: Tenth-century Sufi saint.

Shiva: A name for the all-pervasive supreme Reality.

Shivalingam: Phallic-shaped symbol of Lord Shiva representing the impersonal aspect of God; the symbol by which divine consciousness is worshipped.

Shiva Sutras: Sanskrit text composed of seventy-seven sutras, which Lord Shiva revealed to the sage Vasuguptacharya in order to perpetuate the nondual philosophy.

Shrimad Bhagavatam: A popular devotional scripture sacred to Hindus. especially devotees of Vishnu. It contains legends, stories, and the lives and teachings of the incarnations of Vishnu; composed by Vyasa.

Siddha: Perfected yogi.

Siddharudha Swami: Twentieth-century saint and expounder of Vedanta in whose ashram in Hubli in Karnataka State Swami Muktananda studied as a young monk.

Siddhis: The eight occult powers which the yogi acquires through the practice of yoga.

So'ham (lit. "I am That"): The natural mantra sounded by the breath.

St. John of the Cross: A sixteenth-century Spanish mystic and poet who founded the discalced Carmelites and was author of *The Spiritual Canticle* and *Songs of the Soul*.

Sunderdas (1596-1689): Renowned Indian poet-saint born in Rajasthan; composer of ecstatic poems.

Svetaketu: A figure in the *Chandogya Upanishad*. His father Uddalaka explained to him the mystery of the universal soul.

Tonga: Two-wheeled horse-drawn carriage.

Tukaram Maharaj (1598-1650): Highly popular Maharashtran poet-saint born at Dehu; he was a worshipper of Vitthal.

Tulsidas (1543-1623): North Indian poet-saint; composer of the *Ramacharitamanasa*, the Hindi version of the *Ramayana*.

Turiya: The transcendental state; the fourth state of consciousness beyond waking, dream, and deep sleep, in which the true nature of reality is directly perceived.

Uddalaka: A great Upanishadic sage who expounded the meaning of existence to his son Svetaketu in the *Chandogya Upanishad*.

Vaikuntha: The heavenly abode of Lord Vishnu.

Vasishtha: Ancient sage and Guru of Lord Rama; his teachings are contained in the *Yoga Vasishtha*.

Vedanta (lit. "end of the Vedas"): One of the six schools of Indian philosophy arising from the discussions in the Upanishads about the nature of the Absolute or the Self.

Vedas: The four ancient, authoritative Hindu scriptures; regarded as divinely revealed.

Vijnana Bhairava: Important text of Kashmir Shaivism containing 112 *dharanas* (centering techniques) through which the Absolute is realized.

Vimarsha: Knowledge or awareness; the aspect of consciousness by which all things are known.

Vishnu: The supreme Lord; one of the Hindu trinity of gods representing God as the sustainer; the personal God of the Vaishnavas.

Yajna: Ritualistic sacrifice; any work done in the spirit of surrender to the Lord.

Yajnavalkya: A sage whose teachings are recorded in the *Brihadaranyaka Upanishad*; Guru of King Janaka.

Yoga Vasishtha: A great work on nondual philosophy in which the seer Vasishtha, a son of the Creator, instructs Lord Rama. The theme of the work is that the world is created by the mind.

Yogiraj (lit. "king of yogis"): An honorific title given to advanced practitioners of yoga.

INDEX

220

FURTHER READING

BY SWAMI MUKTANANDA

Play of Consciousness
From the Finite to the Infinite
Where Are You Going?
The Perfect Relationship
Reflections of the Self
Secret of the Siddhas
I Am That
Kundalini
Mystery of the Mind
Does Death Really Exist?
Light on the Path
In the Company of a Siddha
Lalleshwari
Siddha Meditation
Bhagawan Nityananda
Mukteshwari
Meditate

BY SWAMI CHIDVILASANANDA

My Lord Loves a Pure Heart
Kindle My Heart
Ashes at My Guru's Feet

You may learn more about the teachings and practices of
Siddha Yoga Meditation and about books in print by
Swami Muktananda and Swami Chidvilasananda by contacting:

SYDA Foundation
371 Brickman Road, PO Box 600,
South Fallsburg, NY 12779-0600, USA
(914) 434-2000